THE
NATIONAL
PARKS
SCAVENGER
HUNT

Published in 2023 by Timber Press, Inc., a subsidiary
of Workman Publishing Co., Inc., a subsidiary of
Hachette Book Group, Inc.
1290 Avenue of the Americas
New York, New York 10104
timberpress.com

Printed in China on paper from responsible sources
Text design by Adrianna Sutton
Cover design by Adrianna Sutton and Ben Gibson

Library of Congress Cataloging-in-Publication Data

Names: Tornio, Stacy, author.
Title: The National Parks scavenger hunt: a family-friendly way to explore all
    63 parks / Stacy Tornio.
Description: Portland, Oregon: Timber Press, 2023. | Includes bibliographical
    references and index.
Identifiers: LCCN 2022029930 | ISBN 9781643261768 (paperback)
Subjects: LCSH: National parks and reserves–United States–Miscellanea. |
    National parks and reserves–United States–Guidebooks. | Nature study–
    Activity programs. | Outdoor recreation–United States–Miscellanea. |
    United States. National Park Service–Miscellanea.
Classification: LCC E160 .T668 2023 | DDC 333.78160973–dc23/
    eng/20220624
LC record available at https://lccn.loc.gov/2022029930

A catalog record for this book is also available from the British Library.

THE NATIONAL PARKS SCAVENGER HUNT

A Family-Friendly Way to Explore All 63 Parks

INCLUDES **394** FUN-TO-FIND ITEMS

STACY TORNIO

Timber Press
Portland, Oregon

CONTENTS

INTRODUCTION

PUBLIC LANDS ARE INCREDIBLE RESOURCES, allowing all people to visit and experience some of nature's most beautiful places. Congress established the first national park in 1872 in what was then considered the territories of Montana and Wyoming. With this momentous first, Congress stated that Yellowstone National Park should be a "public park for the benefit and enjoyment of the people."

This started an important movement in the United States to protect our nation's natural resources for the future. Later, in 1916, the government established the National Park Service, further designating resources to help keep, maintain, and discover public lands.

Today, 30 states have official national parks. Plus, there are many more national monuments, wildlife refuges, and other important lands throughout the United States. In fact, there are now more than 400 designated areas of the National Park System, making up more than 84 million acres and representing all 50 states.

I'm honored to be writing this scavenger hunt book, featuring our 63 national parks. With each park entry, you'll find many items to look for in a fun scavenger-hunt style. You can read through the entries to learn about these magnificent parks. Then as you visit each one, challenge yourself to find as many items on the list as you can. You might notice that each item is assigned a number of points: 1, 2, or 3. This is to indicate the level of difficulty for each item on the list (1 being the easiest and 3 being the most difficult). Even if you can't check off every item, see how many you can get!

Scavenger hunts are great for all ages, and they've always been a favorite with my own kids. Wherever you go on a hunt, it really makes you look at your surroundings in a different, more inquisitive way. When we're outside, it can be easy to go about our typical day, forgetting to pay attention to the gorgeous scenery around us. I hope this book helps you learn about these parks and find new things to look for and explore as you go out on your adventures.

Have fun exploring our national parks!

EAST

SAILBOAT

RED-BELLIED WOODPECKER

MOSS

LICHEN

CROCODILE

ACADIA
NATIONAL PARK

LOCATION Coastal Maine
SIZE 47,000+ acres
FAMOUS FOR First national park
east of the Mississippi River
ESTABLISHED 1919

12 NUMBER OF ITEMS

POINTS POSSIBLE **24**

YOU'LL GET BOTH MOUNTAINS AND BEACHES when you visit this popular seaside destination. Long before it was a national park, the Wabanaki tribe lived in this area. (Wabanaki translates to "People of the Dawn.") Later in the 19th century, it became a summer hotspot for wealthy families, many of whom worked together to help establish it as a national park. In 1916, the area was designated as a national monument. It became Lafayette National Park in 1919. Then the founder of the park, George B. Dorr, worked to have the park renamed Acadia National Park in 1929. He wrote that the new name was "because of its old historical associations and descriptive character."

SHORT-TAILED WEASEL ○ 3 POINTS

Before you start your search for this small mammal, check the season. Most of the year, this weasel is light brown. Then in winter, it turns as white as snow–during this time, it's known as being "in ermine"–except for the tip of its tail, which stays black year-round. The weasel uses its tail as a distraction technique by whipping it around wildly to keep a predator from attacking.

SEA STAR ○ 2 POINTS

Also called starfish, there are more than 2,000 sea star species around the world. In Acadia, you can often spot sea stars in tide pools during low tide. The two species that exist in this area are the Forbes sea star and the northern sea star. They can be tough to tell apart, but the Forbes species usually have darker orange spots. Both feed on mussels and oysters.

CADILLAC MOUNTAIN ○ 2 POINTS

This famous mountain in Acadia earns the honor of being the highest point along the East Coast at 1,530 feet. The Earth's tectonic and volcanic activity created this mountain millions of years ago. It's a popular area of the park and has amazing views, especially on a clear day. It also has a cool claim to fame. ➡

From roughly October through March, it's the first place in the continental United States where you can see the sunrise. This is because of the way the North Pole is tilted away from the sun in winter.

FERN ○ 1 POINT

Because ferns do best in cool, moist, shaded areas, Acadia makes a great home for them. Several different types of ferns grow in Acadia, including the cinnamon fern. The name comes from the spore-bearing (meaning they produce spores instead of seeds) frond that grows in the middle of the plant—it's cinnamon in color. Try to spot this fern (and the frond) when hiking on the trails.

PEREGRINE FALCON ○ 3 POINTS

The peregrine falcon is the fastest animal in the world, reaching speeds of more than 100 mph when flying and more than 200 mph when diving. Peregrines have been part of the park for many years but stopped nesting in the area during the 1960s and 1970s. This was primarily due to poachers and pesticides, which are both now banned. In 1991, there was finally a new pair of nesting falcons, and they are thriving in the park today!

WHALE ○ 3 POINTS

Whale-watching tours are common throughout the Acadia area, but you can also see these giant beauties from shore. Your chance of success will depend on the time of year and the current state of the water, but summer months are especially good. The four whales you might see are the humpback, minke, pilot, and finback. They'll often swim inland in search of fish. If you do see a finback, consider yourself lucky. It's the second-largest mammal in the world and can reach more than 130 tons and nearly 90 feet in length.

SEAL ○ 2 POINTS

You can see two different types of seals in Acadia: the gray seal and the harbor seal. Look for both of these marine mammals sunning themselves along the park's rocky shorelines. It can be tricky to tell them apart, especially when you're looking from a distance. However, the harbor seal is smaller in size, both in body and the shape of the head. Another fun fact is that the harbor seal will often rest its body in a classic banana shape.

SAILBOAT ○ 1 POINT

If you have the opportunity to explore Acadia by sailboat, then definitely take it. It's an especially popular way to see the famous Mount Desert Island. When you see a sailboat, notice if it has a flag. Flags have long been an important part of the history of sailing. Challenge yourself to find Maine's original state flag, featuring a large green pine tree. You can also look for the newer Maine flag, featuring the state coat of arms on a blue background.

BASS HARBOR HEAD LIGHTHOUSE
○ 1 POINT

This lighthouse on Mount Desert Island is one of more than 80 you can find across Maine. Bass Harbor Head was originally built for $5,000 in 1885. It earned the honor of being on the National Register of Historic Places in 1988 and was featured on the America the Beautiful quarter in 2012. So it's definitely one of the most famous lighthouses in the country.

SAND DOLLAR ○ 3 POINTS

Maine has more coastline than California when you count up all the inlets and bays. This makes Maine and Acadia great places to look for shells and sea life like sand dollars. These little marine animals are closely related to sea stars and sea urchins. While alive and living in water, they're often covered in velvety purple spines. Then they change colors when they wash up on the shore and dry out.

CLIFF ○ 1 POINT

Around Acadia you'll find plenty of cliffs, which were created from the same glacial landforms that made Cadillac Mountain. One of the most famous cliffs both in Acadia and along the East Coast is Otter Cliff. It's 110 feet high and a popular spot for pictures.

ASPEN TREE ○ 2 POINTS

Acadia is made up of a lot of forests that include aspen trees. They are easier to identify than most trees because of their bright white bark. You can find two different types of aspen in Acadia—big-toothed and trembling. Fall is a great time to visit Acadia for the stunning colors, including the golden leaves of aspens.

SHENANDOAH
NATIONAL PARK

LOCATION **Northern Virginia**
SIZE **199,000+ acres**
FAMOUS FOR **Blue Ridge Mountains**
ESTABLISHED **1926**

12
NUMBER OF ITEMS

POINTS POSSIBLE
23

AS THE CLOSEST national park to our nation's capital, this is a popular destination for those who want to escape the city and get out in nature. There are more than 500 miles of trails to explore in this park, including roughly 100 miles of the famous Appalachian Trail. Whether you drive along the park's Skyline Drive (105 scenic miles) or explore the Blue Ridge Mountains, you'll find plenty to see. This national park truly has something for every season. It's especially popular in spring for the waterfalls and in autumn for the fall colors.

WATERFALL ○ 2 POINTS

You can find dozens of waterfalls in Shenandoah National Park, depending on how far you want to hike. The tallest waterfall in the park is Overall Run Falls at nearly 100 feet. One of the most popular and easiest hikes is to Dark Hollow Falls with a height of around 70 feet. Waterfalls often form as streams flow from soft to hard rock; when the soft rock erodes it leaves a hard ledge, which the stream then falls over.

BLACK BEAR ○ 3 POINTS

This is the only bear species in this national park, and thanks to conservation efforts there should be plenty of them for you to try to see (from a safe distance). Many years ago, as few as 10 black bears lived in the park. But as the forests grew and more people worked to protect them, the numbers increased from tens to hundreds. Remember black bears usually go into dens in winter where they are less active. Then they'll come out again, often with cubs, in spring and summer.

HAWK ○ 2 POINTS

The highest point in Shenandoah National Park is called Hawksbill Summit at 4,049 feet. If you drive up to this point, get out and do the 1.7-mile round-trip hike to the viewing platform. Then while you do, challenge yourself to see a hawk. Some of the species you might see include the red-shouldered hawk, sharp-shinned hawk, northern harrier, and northern goshawk. You might find one perched high up in a tree or soaring through the air.

APPALACHIAN TRAIL SIGN ○ 2 POINTS

If you want to hike a famous trail, then look for this sign. It'll point out where you can hike parts of the trail—more than 100 miles of the Appalachian Trail runs through Shenandoah National Park. A man named Earl Shaffer is credited as the founder of this trail. He walked more than 2,000 miles from Georgia to Maine as a form of therapy after serving in World War II.

PARK RANGER ○ 2 POINTS

You can find park rangers at the visitor's center of most national parks. They will have the most up-to-date information and details about things like closed trails, cool sightings, or events happening in the park. Definitely take time to stop to say hi or ask questions. It's one of the best ways to find out what's going on in the area. The first official park ranger dates back to 1905.

MUSHROOM ○ 2 POINTS

You think of most plants as needing sunlight to grow, but not mushrooms. They are fungi after all, not plants. They don't actually contain chlorophyll, so they don't need light or to perform photosynthesis to grow. This means you can easily find mushrooms along trails and deep in the forests. Look for mushrooms in cool, damp spots low to the ground or even growing on trees or logs. Once you're looking for them, they're actually pretty easy to find. But never eat mushrooms unless you have the knowledge or expertise to know which are safe.

OVERLOOK ◯ 1 POINT

Pullouts and overlooks are common in scenic areas all over the country, and that's definitely the case here as well. This national park has more than 70 overlooks where you can stop to admire a majestic view. These are the perfect places to capture great photos or even watch the sunrise or sunset.

SALAMANDER ◯ 3 POINTS

The Shenandoah salamander is a unique and rare species of salamander that can only be found in this national park. It's a lungless salamander, which means it breathes through its skin. This is an endangered species, so it might be challenging to see it specifically. But you can try to see other salamander species, like the spotted, long-tailed, four-toed, and red salamanders. Look for salamanders in damp, swampy areas.

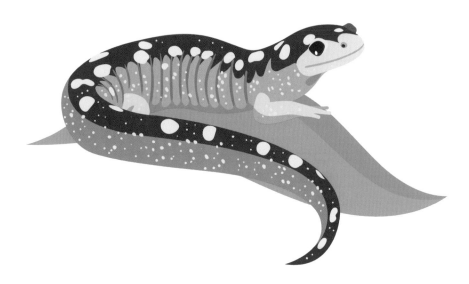

EASTERN REDBUD ○ 2 POINTS

These trees with their bright pink blooms are one of the earliest signs of spring. They often start budding out weeks before other plants, which can be a beautiful sight among a forest of barren trees. If you happen to visit Shenandoah in spring, keep an eye out for the redbud blossoms. During other times of the year, learn to recognize redbuds by their leaves, bark, or other characteristics so you can check this one off your list.

RED-BELLIED WOODPECKER ○ 2 POINTS

You should be able to see several woodpecker species in Shenandoah National Park, including this one. The red-bellied woodpecker's name is tricky because you think you should be able to easily see a red belly, right? It's there but it's not really visible with a quick glance. Instead, look for the black-and-white pattern on its back or the bright red on the back of its head.

BRIDGE ○ 1 POINT

Throughout Virginia, there are many beautiful and classic old bridges. These can be fun to look for as you explore national parks and nature areas. As you go through Shenandoah, look for a bridge while you're along the trails. Better yet, take a photo of it so you can create your own photo scavenger hunt as well.

SUNSET ○ 1 POINT

Did you know that by the time you see the sunset, it's actually gone? That's right. It's a bit of an illusion. By the time those gorgeous colors are shining in the sky, the sun is already below the horizon. Don't forget the time of the sunset changes throughout the year. Check the local time, and then show up about an hour before that time so you can watch the full process.

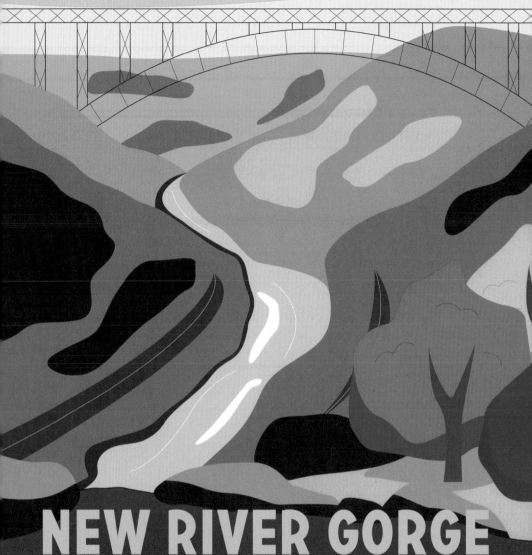

NEW RIVER GORGE
NATIONAL PARK

LOCATION Southern West Virginia
SIZE 70,000+ acres
FAMOUS FOR Bridge going
over the river
ESTABLISHED 2020

7 NUMBER OF ITEMS

POINTS POSSIBLE **12**

THE RIVER THAT RUNS THROUGH THIS NATIONAL PARK,

New River, is one of the oldest rivers on the continent. It flows through several states including this area of West Virginia between the deep canyons. It's a popular area for those who love adventure, and it's common to see kayakers, white water rafters, and rock climbers as you explore the park. Along the river and trails, look for lots of plants, animals, and other great nature moments.

- -

RAVEN ◯ 2 POINTS

Ravens are some of the smartest birds out there. At first glance, you might think a raven is a crow, but it's actually quite a bit larger and has a more distinctive bill. These birds are a bit like acrobats, flying through the air doing somersaults and flips as they go. Young birds will even play a bit of fetch with themselves, dropping a stick in the air and then zooming down to catch it.

OPOSSUM ◯ 2 POINTS

Opossums might not be as cute as raccoons, but these marsupials are fascinating, helpful animals. They can eat thousands of ticks each week–thank you for that! If you see one, look for its incredibly long tail, up to 22 inches. An opossum will use its tail to help itself balance or even carry things.

CLIFF ◯ 2 POINTS

As you go through New River Gorge, you'll likely notice the tall, sandstone cliffs exposed throughout the valley. These have been created from years of erosion, cutting away at the cliff. As you look at them, try to see how many different layers and types of rock you can count. You might even see cliffs with bits of coal.

BRIDGE ○ 1 POINT

The famous bridge in this national park is called the New River Gorge Bridge. It is a classic arched bridge that is more than 3,000 feet long and made from steel. For many years, it was the longest single-span arch bridge in the world—now it's the fifth. This bridge is on the Virginia state quarter, and it's also on the official National Register of Historic Places.

RAPIDS ○ 2 POINTS

New River Gorge attracts thousands of people each year who are looking to float the rapids of the river. With white water rafting, there's a leveling system determined by the International Rafting Federation. These range from Class I (easy) to Class VI (extremely difficult). Most of the rapids in this park fall in Class I, II and III. Some sections can get difficult, so there's really something for everyone!

FOG ○ 1 POINT

Whenever you're in an area with a lot of water, fog is common. A lot of this is steam fog, which happens when cold air moves over warm air. Not everyone loves fog, but it can be very cool and beautiful. So challenge yourself to go out (early morning is best) to capture a cool fog photo in this national park.

RHODODENDRON ○ 2 POINTS

The rhododendron is the state flower of West Virginia. This shrub has earned the nickname of "rose tree" because of the loads of blooms it has in spring. Flowers are usually white, red, purple, or pink. These flowers are often fragrant and very attractive to butterflies, hummingbirds, and bees. If you're visiting this park when these shrubs are no longer blooming, still look for them based on their size and leaf shape.

CUYAHOGA VALLEY
NATIONAL PARK

LOCATION Northeast Ohio
SIZE 32,000+
FAMOUS FOR Natural resources
along the Cuyahoga River
ESTABLISHED 2000

5 NUMBER OF ITEMS

POINTS POSSIBLE 10

CUYAHOGA VALLEY NATIONAL PARK is the only national park in Ohio, located between Akron and Cleveland. It sits along the Cuyahoga River and has a wide range of landscapes, plants, and wildlife. Many people come here for the waterfalls or railroad, only to fall in love with the more than 40 trails throughout the park. It doesn't matter what season you visit this national park because there's always something to see.

WATERFALL ◯ 1 POINT

There are about 100 waterfalls total in Cuyahoga Valley National Park, and one of the most popular is Brandywine Falls. While many waterfalls form because of erosion, they can also be created from volcanoes, earthquakes, landslides, and glaciers.

TRAIN ◯ 2 POINTS

There are 10 national parks that you can reach by train, and this one runs right through the park. Trains have been in this area for more than 100 years, and now you can hop on the Cuyahoga Valley Scenic Railroad for a ride through the national park along the river. It's a great way to experience this area's nature and beauty—look for deer, beavers, birds, and other animals along the way.

MUSKRAT ○ 3 POINTS

Muskrats are a cool water animal. They are amazing swimmers, thanks to their webbed feet, and can go forward and backward and underwater for up to 20 minutes! If you're not sure whether you're looking at a beaver or a muskrat, look at the tail. Muskrats have long, skinny tails and beavers have wide, flat tails.

GREAT BLUE HERON ○ 2 POINTS

Though great blue herons can stand 3 to 4 feet tall, it can be easy to miss them because they're often incredibly still and quiet along the edges of water. They also spend a lot of time fishing and stalking their prey, ready to strike with their powerful bills at any moment. Another good way to see them is to look up and catch a glimpse as they soar from one body of water to another.

BUCKEYE ○ 2 POINTS

The Ohio buckeye is the official state tree of Ohio and also the mascot of the popular Ohio State University. So what is a buckeye exactly? It's the fruit of the tree, and it is brown with a large gray spot—much like a real buck's eye. Many people believe these nut-like fruits can bring you luck, but be aware that they are also highly poisonous.

INDIANA DUNES
NATIONAL PARK

LOCATION Northwest Indiana
SIZE 15,000+ acres
FAMOUS FOR Rolling sandy dunes
ESTABLISHED 2019

5
NUMBER OF ITEMS

POINTS POSSIBLE

12

HERE'S ANOTHER RECENT ADDITION to the National Park System. Indiana Dunes doesn't get as much attention as some of the other national parks in the East, but it's definitely worth a detour along the shores of Lake Michigan. On a clear day your hike up the sandy dunes to the lakeshore will be rewarded with a view of the city of Chicago.

ELEVATION SIGN ◯ 1 POINT

If you go to Indiana Dunes, you'll have the opportunity to take on the "3 Dune Challenge." This involves hiking up three separate dunes for a total of 1.5 miles and 552 vertical feet. If this doesn't sound like much, remember it's all through sand, so it's not as easy as you may think. At the top of each dune, you should see an elevation sign. Don't forget to take a picture!

WARBLER ◯ 3 POINTS

Indiana Dunes is a popular place for birdwatching, and there's a spring bird festival there each year. In particular, warblers are common in the park from spring through early fall. Warblers tend to move around a lot, so they can be tough to spot. Some of the species to look for include the yellow, yellow-rumped, Magnolia, and prothonotary. If you visit this park in late fall through early spring, you won't see warblers, but you can try to find a different bird instead.

GROUND SQUIRREL ◯ 3 POINTS

It's easy enough to see a squirrel in a national park, but seeing a ground squirrel will be more of a challenge. Try to spot a thirteen-lined ground squirrel (also called a striped gopher). It has 13 stripes on its body from shoulder to head. It looks and acts a lot like the common eastern chipmunk, but it's definitely different. Look for the stripes!

OAK TREE ◯ 2 POINTS

Oak trees are incredibly important to wildlife for the way they can provide food and shelter. Within Indiana Dunes National Park, there are black oak savannah areas. Over the years, many of these important habitats have disappeared, so try to appreciate these spots within the park. If you're not sure where to find them, ask a park ranger.

SPIDERWORT ◯ 3 POINTS

Spiderwort is a common wildflower that grows in the woods of this national park. It blooms in spring, usually with blue or purple flowers. These flowers can be short-lived, sometimes only lasting a day, so timing is key to seeing this native plant.

GATEWAY ARCH
NATIONAL PARK

LOCATION St. Louis, Missouri
SIZE 91 acres
FAMOUS FOR Iconic arch
ESTABLISHED 2018

5
NUMBER OF ITEMS

POINTS POSSIBLE
10

EVEN THOUGH IT'S ONE OF THE NEWEST national parks, the Gateway Arch has been an iconic symbol in this area since the 1960s. Located in downtown St. Louis, the "Gateway to the West" is the tallest arch in the world and also the tallest building in Missouri. There might not be miles of trails and wilderness around this national park, but it's an urban treasure with plenty of natural beauty to discover along the Mississippi River.

ARCH ○ 1 POINT

The arch is 630 feet tall and wide, and it took about 2.5 years to build. Because it's made of stainless steel that is hollow inside, you can actually ride in a small tram to a viewing room at the top. On a really clear day, you can see up to 30 miles away. The arch was designated as a National Historic Landmark in 1987, but it didn't become a national park until more than 30 years later.

RIVERBOAT ○ 2 POINTS

Riverboats have long been a common sight on the Mississippi River because they are an easy way to travel up and down this enormous body of water. In particular, they've been common in St. Louis since the construction of the arch. People used to go by the hundreds on these riverboats for the chance to get a closer look at the beautiful arch on the river. Today, you can still see the riverboats from the shore and even book your own trip if you'd like.

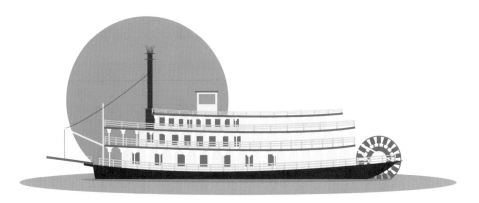

EAGLE ○ 3 POINTS

You can find bald eagles along the Mississippi River throughout the year, but they might be even easier to spot in this area during winter. Eagles like staying along bodies of water like the Mississippi River because there's a ready supply of fish for them to eat. Keep in mind that young (or juvenile) bald eagles don't get their signature white heads until their second or third year. So if you see a bird that looks like an eagle but is all brown, it could just be a young one.

CHERRY TREE
○ 2 POINTS

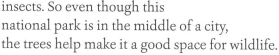

If you visit the arch in spring, especially March or April, then keep an eye out for the blooming cherry blossoms. Planted all around the arch, these trees are a beautiful and fragrant first sign of spring. Cherry trees are also popular with butterflies, hummingbirds, birds, and insects. So even though this national park is in the middle of a city, the trees help make it a good space for wildlife.

BASEBALL ○ 2 POINTS

Do baseballs and national parks go together? They do at this national park. Right next to the Gateway Arch is Busch Stadium, where the St. Louis Cardinals play. You can look right into the stadium from the top of the arch, but even if you don't take the tram ride up, you can still see the stadium. This will increase your chance of seeing a baseball and crossing this scavenger hunt item off your list!

HOT SPRINGS
NATIONAL PARK

LOCATION Hot Springs, Arkansas
SIZE 5,500+ acres
FAMOUS FOR Hot springs
ESTABLISHED 1921

8
NUMBER OF ITEMS

POINTS POSSIBLE
16

THIS NATIONAL PARK goes by the nickname "The American Spa" because of more than 40 thermal springs where half a million gallons of water flow through each day. It's been a highly sought after destination for hundreds of years and was known to Indigenous tribes as a place of peace and healing. Congress established protection for these springs in 1832, long before it was declared a national park and even years before Yellowstone was designated as the first national park in America. With the park tucked in the Ouachita Mountains, there are so many experiences to have and sights to see.

SPRINGS ○ 1 POINT

A natural thermal gradient is at work to heat the water of this national park. The water flows from an area called Hot Springs Mountain at a temperature of about 143°F. While you can't just walk into the water here, there are a couple of places you can feel it directly, so stop at the visitor's center to get tips from a park ranger.

BATHHOUSE ○ 1 POINT

An area called Bathhouse Row in the park includes bathhouses built in the late 1800s and early 1900s. Go here to learn about the thermal water and how important it has been for the area. While most of these bathhouses are now closed, a few are still operating. Make a reservation at one of these bathhouses if you want to experience the hot water of the springs directly!

STRIPED SKUNK ○ 3 POINTS

Don't be afraid of the striped skunk. It's actually a bit challenging to see one because they are nocturnal animals, often coming out around dusk. They tend to mostly keep to themselves and don't spray unless they feel threatened. ➡

If you do happen to smell that oh-so-familiar scent, keep in mind that it can carry up to 1.5 miles. So the skunk might not even be nearby.

TOWER ○ 2 POINTS

The Hot Springs Mountain Tower within the park is an open-air tower more than 1,200 feet above sea level. On a clear day, you could see more than 140 miles all around and also get a good view of the Ouachita Mountains.

CEDAR WAXWING
○ 2 POINTS

Cedar waxwings are birds that are almost always on the move. They will often travel in groups, so if you see one, keep looking because you might see 50 more. This bird gets its name because the very tip of its wing looks like dried red wax. Keep an eye out for these birds in trees with berries—their favorite meal!

RED FOX ○ 3 POINTS

It's not always easy to see a fox because they can be very stealthy as they sneak around looking for food, often at dawn or dusk. One thing you can look for, even if you don't see a fox in person, is their paw prints. Look for both adult-sized prints and younger ones (called pups), as a sign that they're around.

BEE BALM ◯ 2 POINTS

Bee balm is a common wildflower across North America, often growing in swampy areas or near water. You can recognize this plant by the spider-like red, purple, or pink flowers. These plants are excellent for attracting birds, butterflies, bees, and other insects. They are long bloomers, often giving animals a food source from spring through fall.

TENT ◯ 2 POINTS

Tents have been used by different people and cultures for many centuries. The traditional triangle-style tent that is familiar to many of us is called the Sibley tent, and it was invented by the American military officer Henry Hopkins Sibley. He patented the design in 1856. It was originally about 12 feet tall and could fit more than 10 people.

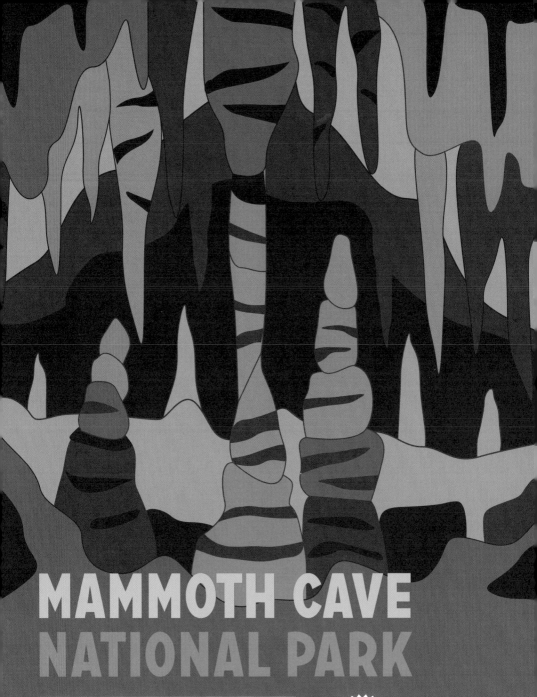

MAMMOTH CAVE
NATIONAL PARK

LOCATION Southcentral Kentucky
SIZE 52,000+ acres
FAMOUS FOR Most extensive
cave system in the world
ESTABLISHED 1941

6
NUMBER OF ITEMS

POINTS POSSIBLE
13

THIS IS THE LONGEST CAVE SYSTEM in the world (at least the longest known one), predicted to have more than 400 miles of underground passageways. It has layers upon layers of limestone, making for very unique shapes and sights that are always changing. This is one of the most unusual national park experiences you can have. You're sure to see things here that you can't spot in any other national park!

- -

STALACTITE ◯ 1 POINT

Stalactites and stalagmites are similar and both are easy to see in Mammoth Cave. They look a bit like icicles, which have formed from water dissolving over the limestone within the cave. Here's a good trick for remembering the difference between the two. Stalagmites have an "m" in the name, and they grow up like mountains from the floor.

FOSSIL ◯ 2 POINTS

Caves provide an excellent environment for fossils, so look for imprints in the rocks when you're underground. Scientists have identified more than 40 shark and shark-like fossils in Mammoth Cave. Ask a park ranger for tips on how and where to see them.

MOSS ◯ 2 POINTS

Moss likes cool, damp areas without direct sunlight. In addition, it can grow on surfaces like bark and rock, so a cave definitely makes a good home for it. Here are two fun facts about moss. First, it doesn't have roots. Second, there are more than 10,000 species of moss around the world.

CRICKET ○ 3 POINTS

Crickets like cool, damp areas. Inside Mammoth Cave, keep an eye out for cave crickets, which are light to dark brown. They have large antennas that are much longer than their bodies. This helps them navigate a cave in the dark and also find food.

KAYAK ○ 2 POINTS

If you want to see Mammoth Cave from a different perspective, consider going on a canoe or kayak tour. You'll paddle the Green River, getting a closer look than you could through a walking tour. It's an underground adventure you'll never forget.

BAT ○ 3 POINTS

Caves have long been an important habitat for animals like bats. For the past several years, a disease called white-nose syndrome has really impacted and threatened the bat community. Conservation groups have been working hard to protect bat species and restore them to places like Mammoth Cave. With many bats sleeping 18 to 20 hours a day, chances are if you see one, it'll be taking a rest.

GREAT SMOKY MOUNTAINS NATIONAL PARK

LOCATION **North Carolina and Tennessee borders**
SIZE **520,000+ acres**
FAMOUS FOR **Smoky Mountains and being the most visited national park**
ESTABLISHED **1934**

12 NUMBER OF ITEMS

POINTS POSSIBLE **20**

YEAR AFTER YEAR, this park earns the top honor of being the most visited national park in the country, hosting more than 10 million visitors annually. It's a huge park at more than half a million acres, so you could spend a week here and still not see it all. Many people come here for hiking, waterfalls, and the chance to see wildlife. What's on your must-see list?

CLINGMANS DOME ○ 2 POINTS

Not only is Clingmans Dome the highest point in the Great Smoky Mountains, but it's also the highest point in Tennessee at 6,643 feet. When you get to the very top viewing spot, you can see more than 20 miles on most days or 100+ miles on really clear days. This observation tower, which is on the National Register of Historic Places, was built in 1959 and has a long ramp of over 300 feet to reach the end.

WATERFALL
○ 1 POINT

You can find many waterfalls here, including the tallest one in the park, Ramsey Cascades. It's actually a tough one to reach though, so be prepared for a challenging hike. Other waterfalls to check out include Indian Creek Falls, which is an easy 1.6 mile hike. You can also look for Rainbow and Hen Wallow Falls.

SALAMANDER ◯ 3 POINTS

About 30 different types of salamanders live in the Great Smoky Mountains, including several in the family of lungless salamanders. Just like their name implies, these little amphibians don't have lungs. Instead, they breathe through their skin. Since salamanders don't have scales, they are a bit slimy. They like damp areas where they can stay moist.

ELK ◯ 2 POINTS

Yes, you can find elk in the East. Once almost completely vanished from this area, these large animals were reintroduced to the national park in 2001. Your best chance to see elk is in the Cataloochee area, which is the southeastern region of the park.

TROUT ◯ 1 POINT

With streams running throughout this national park, you can take a hike along the water and look for fish like trout. As you're looking for trout, there's a good chance you'll also see some people fly fishing. It's a common hobby in this area, and you can even hire your own fishing guide if you want to fish for trout.

MILL ◯ 1 POINT

It really feels like you're going back in time when you visit this area of the national park. The Mingus Mill is a famous historic mill still running in this national park. Built in 1886, this grist mill uses a water-powered turbine. Stop by for a chance to see the mill at work, grinding corn into cornmeal.

BLACK BEAR ◯ 3 POINTS

About 1,500 black bears live within the Smokies so there's a decent chance you can spot one, especially if you're visiting in spring or summer. A lot of people think of black bears as being meat eaters, but their diet is mostly berries and plants. They'll also eat insects or decaying animals.

KINGFISHER ◯ 2 POINTS

Kingfishers are cool birds that love to eat fish and hang out by the water, and the belted kingfisher is the species to look for in the Smokies. You'll definitely know you're looking at a kingfisher because this bird has a head that is bigger than its body. They have large, long bills, and you will often see them perched on a branch along the water as they wait to swoop down to catch their latest meal.

GROUNDHOG ◯ 2 POINTS

The groundhog (aka woodchuck) is one of the most common mammals you'll have the opportunity to see in this national park. These hibernators will go deep into their burrows during winter where they put their bodies into a dormant state. Their burrows can be anywhere from 8 feet deep to more than 60 feet deep.

BLOOMING FLOWER ○ 1 POINT

You can find so many cool plants in the Smokies, including more than 100 native trees, 100 native shrubs, and 1,500 flowers. It's so rich with plant life, you can find something blooming in every season. When you get to the park, stop by the visitor's center or a ranger station to ask what's in bloom. Or take a picture when you're out on the trails so you can get help identifying the plant later.

APPALACHIAN TRAIL SIGN
○ 1 POINT

Here's another national park where you can walk part of the Appalachian Trail. Roughly 70 miles of the trail runs through here. One of the best spots to see a sign and hike part of the trail is at Clingmans Dome.

MAPLE TREE
○ 1 POINT

It should be easy enough to find a maple tree in this national park, but challenge yourself and your family or friends to see who can find the tallest one! If you love tall trees, consider hiking to Albright Grove. It's about a 3-mile trek, but that's where you'll find some of the oldest trees in the park.

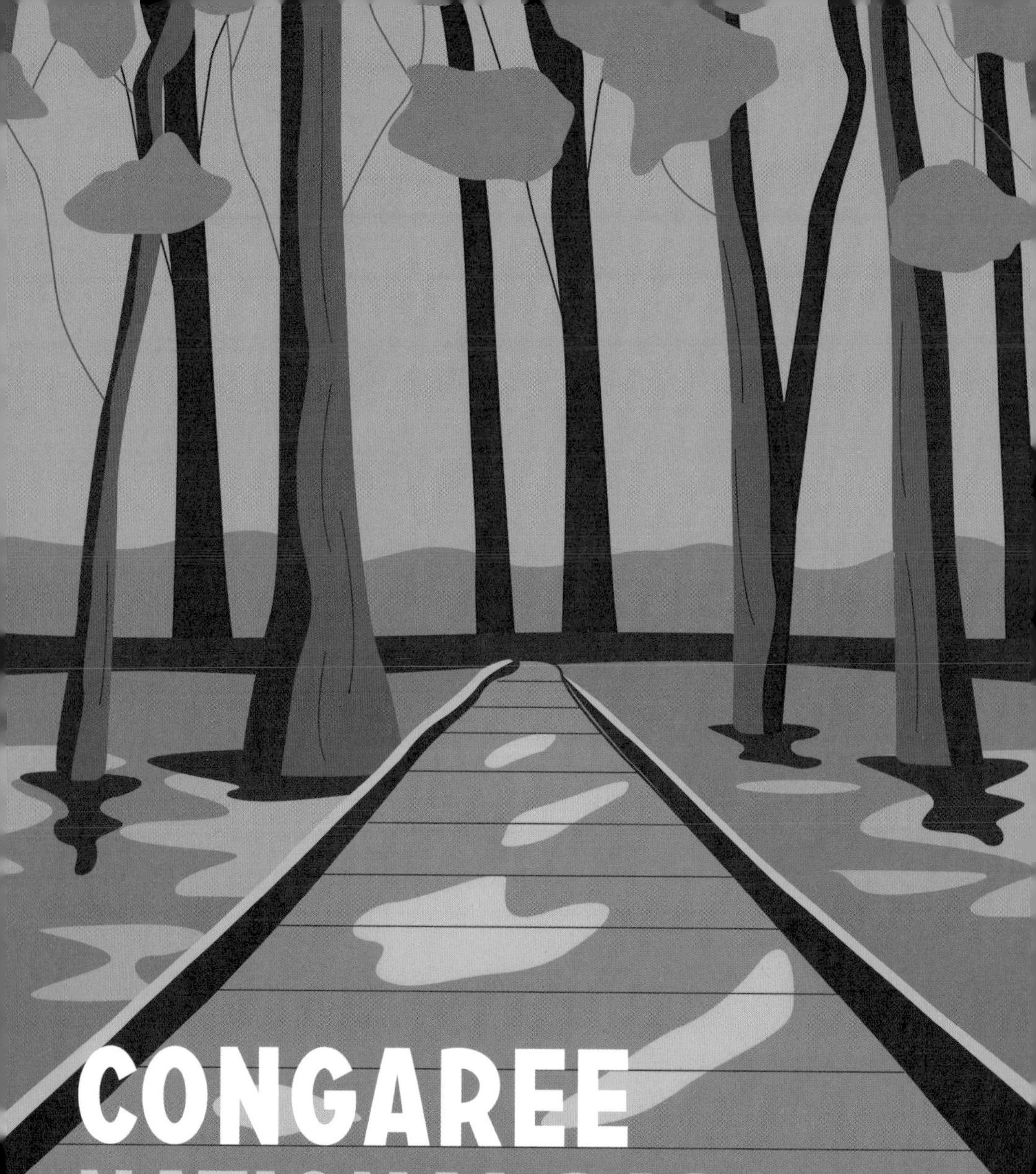

CONGAREE
NATIONAL PARK

LOCATION Central South Carolina
SIZE 26,000+ acres
FAMOUS FOR Largest remaining
area of old-growth bottomland
hardwood forest
ESTABLISHED 2003

5 NUMBER OF ITEMS

POINTS POSSIBLE **9**

CONGAREE IS FULL OF NATURE AND LIFE. As one of the few old-growth forests in the country, it has some of the tallest trees in the eastern half of the United States. Scientists often conduct research and studies in this national park because of the unique combination of plants and wildlife. Since the 1980s, the area has also been designated as an Important Bird Area because of the habitat it provides. Though it's among the least visited national parks, Congaree should be on everyone's list.

BALD CYPRESS
○ 2 POINTS

Bald cypress trees are often associated with the southern swamps of the United States. They have distinctive "knees" that grow up and out from the roots, revealing gaps along the base of the trees. They are in the conifer family, but unlike many conifer trees that keep their needles year-round, they lose theirs each fall and regrow them again in the spring. They can reach heights of more than 100 feet.

BOARDWALK ○ 1 POINT

If you've ever seen pictures of Congaree National Park, there's a good chance you saw a boardwalk in the photo. The boardwalk stretches nearly 2.5 miles into the park, making it a great way to see the giant trees up close. It feels like you're on an escape into the wild.

FIREFLIES ○ 3 POINTS

A famous event involving fireflies happens each spring in Congaree National Park. Often in April, synchronous fireflies show up in the park where they will light up in matching patterns during mating season. It's an amazing, magical sight to witness. But even after this time passes, you can still look for fireflies at night at the park. By the way, there are more than 2,000 different firefly species around the world.

PILEATED WOODPECKER
○ 2 POINTS

Because of all the old-growth trees in Congaree, this is the perfect park to see a lot of different woodpecker species, including the pileated. The pileated is the largest woodpecker you can currently see in America, reaching lengths of 16 to 19 inches. They are about the size of a crow. How many woodpeckers can you spot during a single visit to this park?

WILDFLOWER
○ 1 POINT

Whenever you're in a unique habitat like Congaree with all the swamps and wetlands, you have a chance to see wildflowers you can't see anywhere else. During your trip, try to find a wildflower you've never seen before. Then as an extra challenge, figure out how to identify it (hint: apps and websites can help)!

EVERGLADES
NATIONAL PARK

LOCATION Southern Florida
SIZE 1.5 million acres
FAMOUS FOR Largest subtropical
wilderness in the United States
ESTABLISHED 1934

6
NUMBER OF ITEMS

POINTS POSSIBLE
14

EVERGLADES NATIONAL PARK offers another rare and unique habitat that is home to many species of plants and animals. It's truly one of the wildest lands within the National Park System because much of the park is located in areas that people can't easily access. Scientists predict that more than 30 threatened or endangered species are located here, so it's important to do your part to protect and take care of this park whenever you visit.

MANATEE ◯ 3 POINTS

The West Indian manatee will swim into some Florida waters during winter, including those in Everglades National Park.

These gentle giants can weigh between 1,500 and 1,800 pounds and can live more than 50 years in the wild. They often swim slowly along the bottom of shallow waters, floating up every 15 to 20 minutes to breathe.

CROCODILE ◯ 3 POINTS

Crocodiles are much less common in Florida compared to alligators—about 1,000 crocs across the state compared to more than 1 million alligators. Both are reptiles but come from different families. Crocodiles have longer snouts. Plus, they have the ability to live in both freshwater and saltwater areas, whereas alligators are mostly in freshwater spots.

BROMELIAD ○ 2 POINTS

Bromeliads are a kind of air plant common throughout the Everglades. This type of plant really does grow in the air. It doesn't require any soil, so it often looks like it's floating next to a branch rather than growing on it. They are in the same plant famliy as the pineapple, which makes sense when you see the plant's spiky tops.

ORCHID ○ 3 POINTS

Orchids are delicate flowers that need absolutely perfect conditions to grow outside naturally. Florida and the Everglades have the right habitat in certain areas, which makes for a fun challenge to find an orchid growing in the wild. It won't be easy, but 30+ species have been found here, so keep an eye out!

AIRBOAT ○ 1 POINT

Airboat tours are incredibly popular in the Everglades. In fact, the first airboats to show up in North America were in this area. These flat-bottomed boats are perfect for traveling in the shallow waters, and they can take you to where other modes of transportation can't.

LICHEN ○ 2 POINTS

Lichens are small, slow-growing plants that can form on rocks, trees, and other plants. A cross between fungus and algae, lichens range in color from bright yellow to green to gray. They can be as small as a penny or can even be several feet long! Lichens are a sign of good health for an area, and many animals will use them as food or as nesting materials. They are a favorite choice for hummingbirds when making their tiny nests.

BISCAYNE
NATIONAL PARK

LOCATION Southern Florida
SIZE 172,000+ acres
FAMOUS FOR Islands and coral reefs
ESTABLISHED 1980

5
NUMBER OF ITEMS

POINTS POSSIBLE
12

BEYOND THE CITY LIFE and excitement of Miami sits this incredible national park surrounded by water. From fishing and paddleboarding opportunities to lobstering and snorkeling, there are so many things to do on and around the water. If you love the tropics, then you'll appreciate everything about this park. It gives you that taste of paradise without going too far.

- -

CORAL REEF ○ 3 POINTS

Biscayne is one of the few spots where you can find coral reefs in the continental United States. Within the reefs, there are more than 500 tropical fish and lots of ocean life to discover. With both kayaking and paddleboarding available, seeing the coral reefs for yourself is definitely possible.

SHIPWRECK ○ 3 POINTS

The park has six shipwrecks, so definitely put finding one on your list. There are several tours and boats with clear bottoms, allowing you to get a rare look at these fallen ships. You could also explore them while snorkeling. It's one of the most unique national park experiences you can have.

SEA TURTLE ◯ 3 POINTS

Nearly all sea turtles in the world are considered endangered or threatened in some way, so it's important to protect their habitat however we can. Within Biscayne, the most common species is the loggerhead sea turtle. These turtles grow up to 3 feet long and weigh up to 250 pounds. Females will often return to the sand and beaches where they hatched to lay their own eggs.

MANGROVE ◯ 2 POINTS

Imagine floating through a jungle with trees and leaves surrounding you in the water. This is what a mangrove feels like in Biscayne National Park. Mangroves are made up of multiple trees growing in saltwater, all in the same area. They can line the islands along the coasts, and help protect shorelines from erosion.

FLAMINGO ◯ 1 POINT

Look for these tall pink birds when you're visiting this national park. Biscayne offers a great habitat for flamingos as well as many other tropical-like birds, including pelicans, spoonbills, and cuckoos. The color of flamingos can vary quite a bit because it depends on the carotenoid levels in the algae and crustaceans they eat.

DRY TORTUGAS
NATIONAL PARK

LOCATION West of Key West, Florida
SIZE 64,000+ acres
FAMOUS FOR Historic fort
and coral reefs
ESTABLISHED 1992

5 NUMBER OF ITEMS

POINTS POSSIBLE

11

WITH ITS CLEAR, BRIGHT BLUE WATERS, this national park feels like a tropical paradise. It's located in the Gulf of Mexico, even further west than Key West and is home to many tropical animals and plants, including incredible coral reefs. Also on the island is the famous Fort Jefferson, which was once a prison. It's the largest masonry structure in the Western Hemisphere, made up of more than 16 million bricks.

ISLAND ○ 1 POINT
This park is made up of seven tiny islands: Loggerhead Key, Garden Key, Bush Key, Long Key, Hospital Key, Middle Key, and East Key. You'll easily be able to see these as you arrive on a ferry or when you're out and about, exploring the park. Challenge yourself to find and identify every island within the park.

CORAL ○ 2 POINTS
Did you know there are more than 30 species of coral living underwater at this national park? These marine organisms come in several different shapes and sizes. Go to the local visitor's center to learn about the different types, including elkhorn, staghorn, pillar, lobed star, and rough cactus coral. Then challenge yourself to spot at least three types.

SEA TURTLE ○ 3 POINTS
This area is a popular spot for sea turtles to nest. You can find five different species—the loggerhead, green turtle, leatherback, Kemp's ridley, and hawksbill. These turtles will dig a nest in the sand on the beach, which is sometimes noticeable as a small mound.

Be sure to stay away from these mounds, especially during nesting season (usually spring through fall) because those baby turtles need their space to dig up through the sand so they can crawl out to the sea.

TERN ◯ 2 POINTS

At first glance, you might mistake a tern for a gull, but they are different and have distinct characteristics. Look for their long bills and forked tails. Like gulls, they prefer to travel in groups, so if you see one, you'll likely see a few dozen. Dry Tortugas hosts roughly 300 bird species throughout the year, and terns are one of the few birds that will stay on the islands to nest—not just pass through.

NURSE SHARK ◯ 3 POINTS

Many sharks are hidden within the depths of the ocean, but you can sometimes spot the nurse shark in the shallow, clear waters of Dry Tortugas. Nurse sharks are known as the couch potatoes of the shark world because they tend to be low-key and relatively harmless. They often mate in summer and have their shark babies in winter.

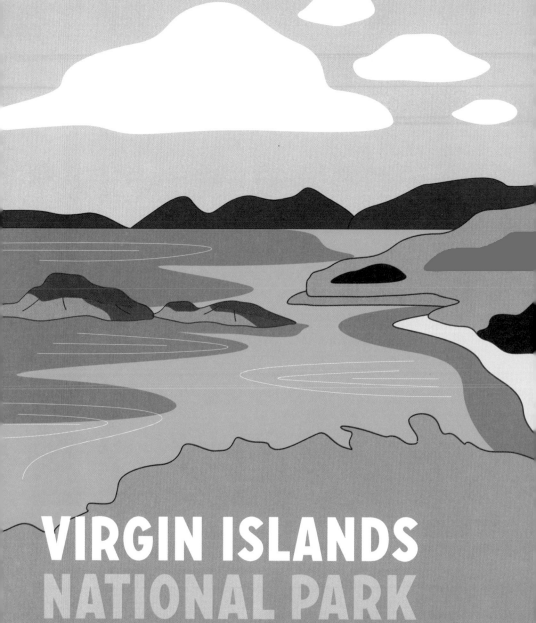

VIRGIN ISLANDS
NATIONAL PARK

LOCATION Virgin Islands
SIZE 14,000+ acres
FAMOUS FOR Being a tropical island
national park
ESTABLISHED 1956

5 NUMBER OF ITEMS

POINTS POSSIBLE **11**

IF YOU'D LIKE TO HAVE MORE sea turtles, beaches, and coral reefs in your life, then add this national park to your list. Located on the island of St. John, this area offers diverse marine life combined with tropical forests. It's one of the more involved national parks to get to, but you'll see some incredible sights and nature while you're there.

- -

SEA TURTLE ○ 3 POINTS

Here's one more national park where you can look for sea turtles, swimming in the water or on the beaches during nesting season.

This national park has an extensive monitoring program, relying on volunteers to help scientists learn more about these awesome reptiles. Two fun facts about sea turtles: they can hold their breath for up to five hours underwater and they also enjoy eating jellyfish.

BAT ○ 2 POINTS

Bats are the only mammals native to Virgin Islands National Park. Yes, there are other mammals on the island now, but they were brought there by humans. Volunteers and researchers monitor the bats to better understand how weather like hurricanes impacts them. Bats can live more than 30 years and fly up to 60 mph, depending on the species!

CACTUS ◯ 2 POINTS

Look for native plants
like cacti in Virgin Islands
National Park. You should
be able to spot the prickly
pear cacti, which has red,
pear-shaped fruit and flat
pads. Both parts of the
plant are edible. If you'd
like to learn how they're
harvested, ask a local on
the island.

STILT ◯ 2 POINTS

You'll be able to see many
shorebirds and tropical birds
across the national park,
including the black-necked
stilt. These tall birds have
long, pink legs, and you'll
often see them wading along
the shoreline looking for
food. Some people refer to
their distinct black-and-
white coloring as a bird tux.

SEA STAR ◯ 2 POINTS

Along the shorelines and in the water, you have the chance to
see so many cool tropical fish and species, including the sea star.
Look for the cushion sea star, which tends to have a puffy, pillow-
like appearance. Sea stars can live up to 35 years in the wild.
Remember these cool creatures need to stay in the water (and
don't survive in freshwater), so observe and take pictures, but let
them be.

MIDWEST

PONDEROSA PINE

BLACK-FOOTED FERRET

SANDHILL CRANE

LOON

MILKWEED

VOYAGEURS
NATIONAL PARK

LOCATION Northern Minnesota
near the Canadian border
SIZE 200,000+ acres
FAMOUS FOR Wild areas and waterways
ESTABLISHED 1975

7 NUMBER OF ITEMS → POINTS POSSIBLE **14**

THIS PARK MIGHT NOT SEE A LOT OF VISITORS, but those who do make it to Voyageurs truly feel like they have discovered a hidden gem. Located in far northern Minnesota, this park is particularly popular in summer, especially among people who love to canoe, kayak, or boat. Most of this national park is only accessible by boat. People who enjoy remote areas love this national park.

- -

MOOSE ◯ 3 POINTS

It's not going to be easy to spot a moose at this national park, but it's a good challenge! Your best opportunity will be to go hiking near water areas, either early in the morning or early in the evening. These large mammals like to stay near the water where they eat plants and go swimming. They love the water and can spend up to two hours at a time swimming. They can even stay underwater for as long as 30 seconds at a time.

LOON ◯ 2 POINTS

The common loon is the state bird of Minnesota. During peak breeding season in summer, they have bold black-and-white markings and deep red eyes. You might think a loon is much like a duck, but scientists say that they are actually more closely related to penguins. If you visit this national park in the summer, look for a loon. Try to spot a young one as well. They might be swimming alongside their parents or sometimes even sitting on their backs!

NORTHERN LIGHTS ◯ 3 POINTS

This national park is one of the few places in the United States where you can see the northern lights during certain times ➡

of the year. Northern lights can actually be shining at any time, but it needs to be dark in order to see them. Here are two cool facts about northern lights—scientists say they can be visible from space and that other planets have them as well!

MUSHROOM
◯ 1 POINT

Mushrooms have so many nutritional benefits. For instance, they can have more potassium than a banana and can be a great source of Vitamin B. Many people believe mushrooms even have healing powers for things like cancer. Since mushrooms don't need sunshine to grow, you can find them in many damp, wooded areas. Before you eat any you find, check with a ranger or a trusted source to make sure they're not poisonous.

MILKWEED ◯ 2 POINTS

There are more than 70 species of milkweed throughout North America. While this plant is best known as a host plant for monarchs (who lay their eggs on it so when caterpillars hatch they can eat it), milkweed leaves, sap, and nectar are also a good food source for other butterflies and insects as well. The next time you see milkweed in the wild, take a closer look. You might see a little creature stopping for a bite to eat.

KAYAK ◯ 1 POINT

The first known kayaks were built by the native Inuit and Aleut people in the Arctic. They created them mostly for the purpose of hunting. Because of the way the boats were designed, they could move quickly and quietly in the water to sneak up on animals. Plus, they could travel through shallow areas, allowing them to go through waterways that other boats couldn't.

EAGLE ◯ 2 POINTS

Bald eagles are excellent fliers and hunters. They can fly up to 30 mph while in their regular flight, but they can move as fast as 100 mph when diving to pursue prey! When bald eagles nest, the young might stay in their nests for a few months before they start going out independently. Even then, though, their parents will keep feeding them for a few more months before they are truly on their own.

ISLE ROYALE
NATIONAL PARK

LOCATION Upper Michigan
near Minnesota
SIZE 570,000+ acres
FAMOUS FOR More than 400
wild islands
ESTABLISHED 1940

5 NUMBER OF ITEMS

POINTS POSSIBLE **8**

THIS NATIONAL PARK is in the state of Michigan, but it's really close to Minnesota and also to Canada. The main island is more than 45 miles long, making it one of the largest lake islands in the world. There are also about 400 tiny nearby islands, which create a really unique ecosystem and national park. You'll want to plan a trip to this park in the summer when the ferry is running. This is another park that is truly off the beaten path. It's an experience you'll never forget!

WOLF ○ 3 POINTS

Have you ever heard of the phrase wolf pack? Wolves will often gather together in a group, called a wolf pack, and this is how they sleep, hunt, and live. This means if you see one wolf, there's a good chance others are nearby. Wolves are often on the move, traveling as much as 8 miles or more every single day.

SANDHILL CRANE
○ 2 POINTS

Sandhill cranes are hard to miss in the wild. Reaching up to 4 to 5 feet, these gentle giants really stand out, whether they're in flight or fishing along the edge of the water. If you're in Isle Royale during summer, keep an eye out for crane nests. They build them on the ground in marshes or wetlands. Once babies are born, they often start swimming within a few hours. They will stay with their parents for several months before they are completely on their own.

FERN ◯ 1 POINT

Did you know ferns are some of the oldest living things that exist on our planet? It's true. There's evidence that says they've been around since before the dinosaurs. You can find more than 10,000 species of ferns all around the world. The bracken fern is a common species that you can find in this park. For a more rare species, look for the moonwort, which has moon-shaped leaflets.

LICHEN ◯ 1 POINT

Lichens can grow almost anywhere in the wild including living trees, fallen logs, and rocks. A fun challenge is to see how many different places you can find lichen growing. Because lichens absorb the air and water around them, their coloring can be a big indication of the health of the surrounding environment.

CANOE ◯ 1 POINT

This national park isn't too far from the famous Boundary Waters Canoe Area Wilderness. This is an area of more than 1 million acres in the Superior National Forest in Minnesota. Adventurers come from all over the world to canoe here, so naturally, this hobby stretches into this national park as well. While you're at the park, try to see how many different types of watersports you can see.

THEODORE
ROOSEVELT
NATIONAL PARK

LOCATION Western North Dakota
SIZE 70,000+ acres
FAMOUS FOR Being named after the
26th president of the United States
ESTABLISHED 1978

5 NUMBER OF ITEMS

POINTS POSSIBLE
9

GET A TASTE FOR THE WEST as you travel through Theodore Roosevelt National Park. The wild and wide open space is home to animals like bison and wild horses. It's not hard to imagine why Indigenous peoples roamed the lands of this park, hunting and exploring. President Teddy Roosevelt used to come to this area to hunt bison when he was young. Between the miles of hiking trails and scenic drives, you'll have plenty to explore during your trip.

BISON ◯ 2 POINTS

Bison could have easily become extinct if it weren't for federal legislation in 1894 that finally helped protect them. Slowly, they started increasing in population again. In 1956, around 29 bison were released in the South Unit of this national park. In less than 10 years, this herd had increased to more than 145 animals. Now, it's common to see these animals wandering around the park.

PRAIRIE DOG ◯ 2 POINTS

You can find five species of prairie dogs in North America, but the only one you'll find in this national park is the black-tailed. These animals, which are part of the rodent family, grow to be about 12 to 15 inches tall. They stick together in a group, called a coterie, and live underground in burrows.

WESTERN MEADOWLARK
◯ **3 POINTS**

This beautiful yellow-and-black flier is the official state bird of Kansas, Montana, Nebraska, North Dakota, Oregon, and Wyoming. They like open areas where they can perch on trees, fence posts, or wires to feed on insects and bugs. They will nest on the ground near fields and grasslands.

CABIN ◯ **1 POINT**

As you pass through this national park, be sure to stop to see the famous Maltese Cross Cabin. Theodore Roosevelt used to stay in this cabin before he was president, and it's on display at the visitor's center. It's built out of pine logs and has three separate rooms—a kitchen, living room, and bedroom.
This was pretty luxurious back in the day!

CANYON ◯ **1 POINT**

Going to Painted Canyon is a must when you visit this national park. The name of the canyon comes from the many layers you can see in the rocks. The popular Painted Canyon Overlook includes several options for hiking. It's the perfect way to get to know the area.

BADLANDS
NATIONAL PARK

LOCATION Southwest South Dakota
SIZE 240,000+ acres
FAMOUS FOR The Badlands
ESTABLISHED 1978

5
NUMBER OF ITEMS

POINTS POSSIBLE
11

BETWEEN THE FOSSILS, BISON, AND AMAZING STARS

you can see at night, this national park is a can't-miss stop during your travels out West. You can't really explain the landscape of the Badlands . . . you just have to experience it for yourself. As you gaze across the canyons of this national park, there's always something new to see among the layers of rocks and terrain. Every year, it attracts fossil admirers because you really can see them just by taking a hike through the park. Be sure to stop in the visitor's center to learn more about this unique area.

- - - - - - - - - - - - - - - - - - - -

BISON ○ 1 POINT

The bison is the largest land animal in North America. Males (aka bulls) can weigh more than 2,000 pounds while the females weigh around 1,000 pounds. The big hump you see on a bison is actually made of muscle. This allows it to push heavy things around such as snow!

BIGHORN SHEEP
○ 2 POINTS

Both male bighorn sheep (called rams) and females (ewes) have horns, though the male's horns are bigger and more prominent. Rams start growing their horns at birth and continue growing them throughout their lifetime. The rings in the curved horns of the male ram represent their overall age. A status symbol in the animal world, the horns can also be used as a weapon. All in all, a male's horns can weigh up to 30 pounds!

BLACK-FOOTED FERRET
○ **3 POINTS**

Black-footed ferrets were
believed to be extinct in 1980.
However, thanks to conservation
efforts in the 1990s, this little
mammal is alive and well in
the Badlands today. They are
considered one of the most
endangered mammals in North America, and this is one of the few
areas where you can see them. They've lost a lot of habitat over the
years, but they will use old prairie dog burrows for their homes.
Black-footed ferrets mostly come out at night, so it might be hard
to spot them. However, if you check with a ranger, they should be
able to give you some tips.

BURROWING OWL
○ **2 POINTS**

A lot of people think of owls as being
nocturnal, and in many cases, this is
true. However, burrowing owls are
active during the day as well because
they're out looking for insects and small
mammals to eat. Unlike many owls you
find in trees, these are most commonly
spotted on the ground. Their burrows
can be 10 feet deep or more.

FOSSIL ○ **3 POINTS**

This national park attracts fossil hunters
from all over the world who are eager to
see ancient history captured in the rocks
and soil. You'll find plenty of fossils on
display throughout this area, but the real
challenge is to get out there and find one
for yourself while hiking and exploring
the park. Stop at the visitor's center for
tips, and then happy hunting!

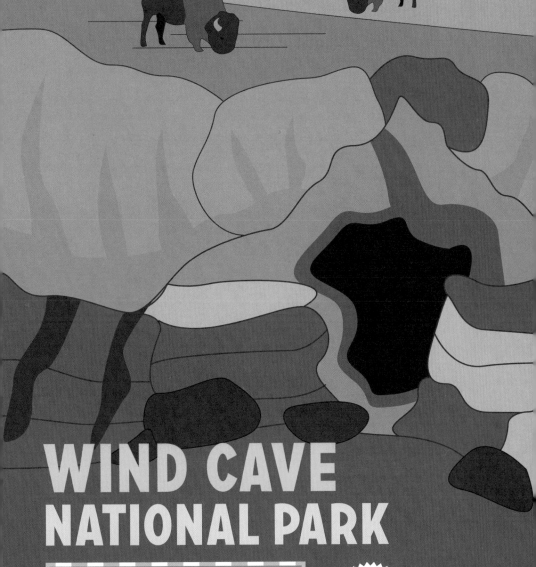

WIND CAVE
NATIONAL PARK

LOCATION Southwest South Dakota
SIZE 33,000+ acres
FAMOUS FOR Enormous cave
ESTABLISHED 1903

5
NUMBER OF ITEMS

POINTS POSSIBLE
10

THIS IS ONE OF THE EARLIEST national parks, established in 1903. The cave here is an example of boxwork, which is a formation that has unique honeycomb box patterns. You'll definitely want to go underground for a cave tour while you're here. There are also plenty of sites to see above ground as well. Throughout this beautiful public land, you'll find a mix of prairies and forests, which are home to wildlife like bison, pronghorn, and other grassland species.

PRAIRIE FALCON ○ 3 POINTS

The prairie falcon is similar in size to the peregrine falcon, though it's mostly found in the West. You can often see them nesting high up on the cliffs or in canyons, yet they spend a lot of time flying low to the ground. This is a hunting technique for them. They will fly low to sneak up on and surprise prey. They can fly up to 45 mph and can dive at speeds of more than 100 mph.

PONDEROSA PINE
○ 2 POINTS

Hiking to the highest point of Wind Cave means traversing through the beautiful ponderosa pine forests. The ponderosa pine has a deep root system, making it a good wind-resistant tree. It can easily reach more than 100 feet, and many people say it has a sweet scent.

PURPLE CONEFLOWER
○ 2 POINTS

No matter what national park you visit, it's a good habit to look for native wildflowers because you'll learn a lot about the area. The purple coneflower is a native flower you can find at Wind Cave National Park. Also called echinacea, these pink wildflowers are great for birds, bees, and butterflies. They're also popular in home and public gardens, so they might look familiar when you spot them in the wild.

PRONGHORN ○ 2 POINTS

Pronghorns are unique because they are only found in North America. Some people call them antelope, but they are actually different from antelopes and are even more closely related to giraffes! Every fall, pronghorns shed their horns, but they grow back by summer.

CAVE ○ 1 POINT

Yes, the cave at this national park can get quite windy! This is because it's a really big cave with a lot of space. Therefore, it has an air pressure system. Depending on the air pressure outside of the cave and at the surface, it can be quite different and cause wind. The wind within this cave system has been clocked at more than 70 mph!

MOUNTAIN WEST

GRIZZLY BEAR

LONGS PEAK

GRAY WOLF

COLLARED LIZARD

WESTERN TANAGER

FRINGED GENTIAN

BLACK-CHINNED HUMMINGBIRD

GLACIER
NATIONAL PARK

LOCATION Northwest Montana
SIZE 1+ million acres
FAMOUS FOR Glaciers, lakes,
and mountain landscapes
ESTABLISHED 1910

10
NUMBER OF ITEMS

POINTS POSSIBLE
17

WITH ACRES AND ACRES of rugged landscape and more than 600 miles of hiking trails, this is truly one of the most wild parks in the Lower 48. This national park is on the border of Montana and Canada, and it's also part of the larger Waterton-Glacier International Peace Park. As you travel through the park, it's pretty amazing to think of the glaciers from millions of years ago that have formed the mountains, valleys, and lands of this national park. There are still some glaciers left today, though scientists aren't sure how many more years they will last. Put it on your list to visit soon, and plan for several days to see it all!

MOUNTAIN GOAT
○ **2 POINTS**

Look up if you want to see a mountain goat at Glacier. While you might see these mammals along the trails, it's more likely that you'll see them high upon the cliffs or on the mountains. Their cloven hooves feel almost like sandpaper, which is what allows them to climb up rough terrain. Reaching these remote areas helps keep them safe from predators like mountain lions or bears.

BEAR ○ **2 POINTS**

You could spot both black and grizzly bears in this national park. Keep in mind that bears can be a safety issue, especially during certain times of year. But as with most wildlife, you'll be fine if you keep your distance. So how can you tell the difference between the two? Grizzlies are much bigger overall and have brown, rough fur.

HARLEQUIN DUCK
○ **3 POINTS**

It's not going to be easy to see a harlequin duck, but if you do, you won't forget it for a very long time. Many people call this duck a clown duck because of its unique, clown-like markings. They are typically a sea duck, so this is among the rare places you can see one in the Lower 48. Look for them diving underwater as they search for food.

GOLDEN-MANTLED GROUND SQUIRREL ○ **1 POINT**

This squirrel looks a lot like a chipmunk at first, but it doesn't have a stripe on its head and it has a shorter tail. It's also much bigger than most chipmunks, up to a foot long. This is a common squirrel in the West, and is also found in national parks like Rocky Mountain and Yellowstone. Watch for these little rodents gathering nuts in preparation for winter.

BEARGRASS ○ **2 POINTS**

This plant isn't actually a grass at all, but a flower within the lily family. It's native to Montana and the Pacific Northwest. It grows up to 5 feet tall and has pretty white flowers at the top. Animals like sheep, mountain goats, and elk will eat the plant, which grows in rocky terrain.

CONTINENTAL DIVIDE
○ **2 POINTS**

The Continental Divide is an epic hydrological divide that runs from Alaska through South America. Around 110 miles of this famous divide goes through Glacier National Park, so it's a cool experience to hike a piece of the trail. For those who want a challenge, find the place in the park called the Glacier's Triple Divide Peak. Water from this rare split will eventually flow into three different areas—the Atlantic Ocean, the Pacific Ocean, and Hudson Bay.

RED BUS ◯ 1 POINT

Even if you don't ride on a red bus yourself, then at least look for them as you travel through the park. These historic buses from the 1930s have roll-back tops that allow passengers to get great views from all angles. They may not be roomy or modern, but they certainly are a historic and unique experience.

LAKE ◯ 1 POINT

Because of the glaciers that have been here for millions of years, there are many bodies of water to see. Glacier National Park has more than 700 lakes, but only about 131 of them have names. Lake McDonald is the biggest and deepest lake at the park, reaching 10 miles long and more than 450 feet deep.

LOGAN PASS ◯ 2 POINTS

This is one of the most popular areas of the park and is also home to two popular hiking trails, including Hidden Lake Trail and Highline Trail. It's right along the Continental Divide and is the highest point in the park at 6,700 feet. Plan to go early or to take a shuttle for the best experience.

RAFT ◯ 1 POINT

The waters of Glacier attract some of the most adventurous white water rafters in the world. Look for rafts in all areas of the national park. Then if you're up for the challenge, find an adventure company and book an experience at the right level for you. This is truly a one-of-a-kind national park experience!

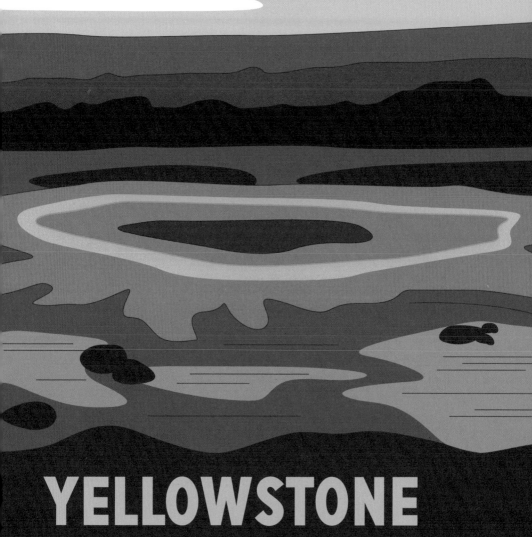

YELLOWSTONE
NATIONAL PARK

LOCATION Northwest Wyoming and
parts of Montana and Idaho
SIZE 2.2+ million acres
FAMOUS FOR The first national park
ESTABLISHED 1872

12
NUMBER OF ITEMS

POINTS POSSIBLE
24

SEE THE MAGIC of the country's first national park for yourself when you head out West to Yellowstone. This national park protects the largest concentration of geysers and geothermal features in the world and is also home to the famous Old Faithful. The park is a true wilderness paradise with more than 900 miles of trails to explore. Each year, millions of people come here to camp, hike, and explore the wonders of nature. Between fishing, rafting, hiking, and wildlife watching, you'll need several days to see it all!

BEAR ○ 3 POINTS

There are two different types of bears you could see in Yellowstone–black bear or grizzly bear. One way to tell the difference is that grizzlies tend to have a bit of a hump on the back of their neck but black bears do not. You can also look at the bear tracks. Grizzly tracks have longer claws and toes closer together whereas black bear tracks have shorter claws and more separated toes.

GRAY WOLF ○ 3 POINTS

During the mid 1900s, wolves were disappearing all across North America, including in Yellowstone. However, thanks to restoration efforts, gray wolves are now common in Yellowstone once again. Right now, scientists estimate there are more than 500 wolves in the park. They tend to travel in packs of about 10, hunting and living together.

SQUIRREL ○ 1 POINT

You can find several different squirrel species in Yellowstone, including the common red squirrel. Red squirrels tend to look a lot like gray squirrels, though they are about half the size. Other squirrels you can look for in the park include the golden-mantled ground squirrel, which looks a lot like a chipmunk, and the northern flying squirrel.

TROUT ○ 2 POINTS

Fishing and trout go hand in hand at Yellowstone. Anglers from all over the world come to fish the streams of this famous national park. They'll often be fly fishing specifically for trout. The Yellowstone cutthroat trout, which is native to the park, is an important fish in the area because it provides food to a lot of different wild animals.

GEYSER ○ 2 POINTS

You can find many geysers in Yellowstone National Park, and two of the most famous ones are Old Faithful and Steamboat Geyser. Old Faithful has very predictable eruptions, and you can often find a schedule of when it's expected to go off next. Steamboat is less predictable but bigger. It's actually the world's tallest geyser.

MOUNTAIN GOAT ○ 2 POINTS

Mountain goats aren't native to Yellowstone, but they've been there ever since they were introduced to the area in the 1940s. Male mountain goats (billies) are about twice the size of females (nannies). Both have horns, though the female's horns are thinner and don't curve as much.

FRINGED GENTIAN ○ 3 POINTS

Not all national parks have an official flower, but Yellowstone does. This beautiful wildflower blooms in summer and has deep purple flowers with fringed edges. This plant isn't super common, but if you are visiting in late June or July, try to check it off your list!

BISON ○ 1 POINT

Yellowstone is home to the country's largest bison population. It's a huge herd with thousands of individuals. You can find them throughout the park as they feed on grasses and sedges. Even though it seems like these animals are gentle giants, it's important to remember to never approach them or any other wildlife in the park.

WATERFALL ○ 1 POINT

You can hike to plenty of waterfalls in Yellowstone. For instance, Tower Fall is one of the most famous where you can watch the water flow into the Yellowstone River. Lower Yellowstone River Falls is even more famous and has a 308-foot drop. Kepler Cascades is perfect if you want something off the beaten path.

TRUMPETER SWAN ○ 2 POINT

There are only a handful of trumpeter swans in Yellowstone, but you can't miss their beautiful, elegant necks and striking black bills. These birds are known to mate for life, which is a bit rare in the bird world. The same swan couples will come together year after year to raise their family.

FROG ○ 2 POINTS

The boreal chorus frog is the one you'll be looking for in Yellowstone—or rather, listening for. These amphibians are seldom seen but often heard. This small frog is only about 3 inches wide. They come together at the water in spring where the males call out repeatedly in order to attract a female.

PETRIFIED TREE ○ 2 POINTS

Stop at the visitor's center to ask where you can find petrified trees in Yellowstone. Also called Fossil Forest, this area is home to trees from millions of years ago. It's pretty cool to be able to say you saw a fossil while in Yellowstone!

GRAND TETON
NATIONAL PARK

LOCATION Northwest Wyoming
SIZE 300,000+ acres
FAMOUS FOR Teton mountains
ESTABLISHED 1929

8 NUMBER OF ITEMS

POINTS POSSIBLE **16**

GRAND TETON NATIONAL PARK is only a hop, skip, and a jump away from Yellowstone. Once people discover this gem, they often prefer it over Yellowstone because it's smaller and less crowded (and therefore, easier and faster to travel). You can see the rugged, snow-capped Teton Range for miles away on a clear day. This park is popular for those looking for close-up experiences with wildlife. It really does offer a remote, wild look at the world.

- -

RIVER OTTER ○ 3 POINTS

It's not always easy to see a river otter in the wild, but you'll have a good chance when visiting Grand Teton National Park. These little mammals are mostly nocturnal, so wake up early in the morning to try to spot one. Look for them floating and swimming near the surface of ponds, lakes, and rivers. River otters can hold their breath for up to 8 minutes underwater!

MOOSE ○ 3 POINTS

If seeing a moose is on your bucket list, then Grand Teton National Park is a great place to go. Scientists estimate that more than 800 moose live in the area, and you can check with a local park ranger to get tips on where to look. A fun fact about moose young (called calves) is that they grow fast and can outrun a person after just 5 days.

WILLOW

○ **1 POINT**

Willow trees are common throughout Grand Teton National Park, so learn how to recognize the long, thin leaves so you can properly identify one.

Willows are an important food source for moose. In fact, willows make up nearly all of their summer diet. This is a good tip if you're looking for a moose. First find some willow trees, and you're likely to find a moose not too far away!

WESTERN TANAGER ○ **3 POINTS**

You'll have to visit Grand Teton National Park in summer if you want to see this bright and beautiful bird. The western tanager is about the size of an American robin, and you can't miss the male species with their fiery colors. (Females are more yellow and olive green overall.) It looks like a tropical bird and will nest in the trees of the surrounding forests. It's not going to be easy to see one, but if you get the timing right, consider yourself lucky!

SNOW ○ **1 POINT**

You can find snow in Grand Teton National Park pretty much year-round. Even if you don't walk on the snow yourself, you'll probably see it in the distance on the mountains. This area sees about 150 to 175 inches of snow in the valley; up on the mountains, there's easily more than 500 inches of snow. Not surprisingly, skiing is a popular winter activity in the nearby town of Jackson Hole.

ELK ◯ 2 POINTS

You could see the largest elk herd in North America when you visit Grand Teton National Park. This herd splits its time between the park and a nearby elk refuge. If you don't see an elk, then at least listen for them. They have a bugle call that can carry for miles!

JENNY LAKE ◯ 1 POINT

Jenny Lake is a popular destination in Grand Teton National Park. It was formed roughly 12,000 years ago by glaciers. From here, you can hike the trail to Grand Teton, the tallest peak of the Teton mountains. You can also take the challenge of hiking around the lake, which is a roughly 7-mile trek.

MOUNTAIN CHICKADEE ◯ 2 POINTS

Chickadees are common birds all around the country, with the black-capped and Carolina chickadees being more prevalent in the East. The mountain chickadee is more common in the West and mountainous regions. They feed on insects, seeds, and berries, and you can usually spot them in conifer trees.

ROCKY MOUNTAIN
NATIONAL PARK

LOCATION **Northcentral Colorado**
SIZE **265,000+ acres**
FAMOUS FOR **Epic mountains**
ESTABLISHED **1915**

8 NUMBER OF ITEMS

POINTS POSSIBLE **15**

ROCKY MOUNTAIN NATIONAL PARK is one of the most visited national parks in the country. From the majestic mountain peaks to the abundance of wildlife, you'll always have something to see. Plus, it's just a short drive (about 1.5 hours) from Denver. Trail Ridge Road, which leads up the mountain and then back down, makes it an easy park to access. Whether you're looking to hike 10+ miles or watch for wildlife from the car, you can do it all in this park.

- -

BEAVER ○ 2 POINTS

Beavers are incredible creatures with many talents. If you want to see one, look near the water, especially where there are streams. They build homes (also known as dams) and sometimes live in groups called lodges. These mammals have waterproof fur and are incredible swimmers. They can even stay underwater for up to 20 minutes.

ASPEN ○ 1 POINT

You can't miss aspen trees while going through the Rockies. They are everywhere and easy to recognize with their pale white bark. Aspens have distinct round or oval leaves with rough edges. In the fall they change from green to a beautiful gold color. The bark of these trees is often used to make medicine.

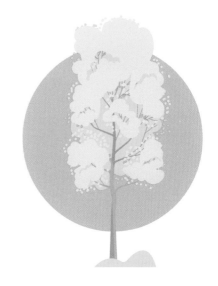

CONTINENTAL DIVIDE ○ 2 POINTS

Want the opportunity to say you hiked a famous trail? Stop at the Continental Divide while in Rocky Mountain National Park. You can hike roughly 28 miles of this trail in the park, and you'll have so much to see along the way. Ask a ranger for tips if you want to hike part of the trail!

ELK ○ 1 POINT

In peak summer months, there could be as many as 3,200 elk in Rocky Mountain National Park. In winter, their number drops to about 800. Each winter, male elk will drop their antlers. Then in spring, they start growing back and can grow as much as an inch every day. These social animals will travel in groups of dozens or even a hundred or more!

BEAR LAKE
○ 2 POINTS

Bear Lake is one of the most popular destinations in the Rockies. This beautiful lake often shows up in pictures of this national park. Many people enjoy hiking around the lake for a real Rocky Mountain experience. The parking lot almost always fills before 9 am, so plan to take the shuttle or wake up early.

AMPHITHEATER ○ 2 POINTS

Moraine Park Amphitheater is a lovely outdoor theater built in the 1930s. It's a great place to stop for a photo or to explore a different side of this national park. There is some debate as to when the first amphitheater was created, but it definitely dates back as far as Pompeii in 75 BCE.

LONGS PEAK ○ 2 POINTS

Longs Peak is the tallest peak in the Rockies (14,259 feet) and it is visible from pretty much everywhere in the park. It's also a popular peak for experienced hikers and climbers to summit. You can find a trail cam for this area on the National Park Service's website, but make sure you see it in person as well—at least from a distance!

AMERICAN DIPPER ○ 3 POINTS

The American dipper is nearly always near a stream. Not only does it nest alongside water, but it also catches nearly all of its food in the water. In fact, this bird has impressive skills when it comes to hunting... or fishing actually. It catches its food underwater, even in rushing water, by swimming or walking along the bottom!

GREAT
SAND DUNES
NATIONAL PARK

LOCATION Southcentral Colorado
SIZE 42,000+ acres
FAMOUS FOR Tallest sand dunes
in North America
ESTABLISHED 2004

6 NUMBER OF ITEMS

POINTS POSSIBLE **13**

YOU'LL HAVE TO SEE THESE DUNES in person to truly appreciate them. The tallest one in this park is 750 feet, which makes it North America's tallest dune. In 1932, this area became a national monument, which helped it receive federal protection. This also helped protect the grasslands, wetlands, and other habitats in the area. It finally earned the honor of becoming a national park in 2004.

- -

DUNE ◯ 1 POINT

It's hard to miss seeing a dune while in this national park, but it should still be on the list. Scientists estimate these dunes started forming more than 400,000 years ago when a large lake in the area dried up. Because of the way the area is formed with two mountain streams nearby, there is always sand movement happening, which helps keep the dunes preserved.

TIGER SALAMANDER ◯ 3 POINTS

This isn't going to be easy, but it's worth keeping an eye out for the tiger salamander. It has a unique spotted pattern with green or yellow stripes across its brown or black skin. They spend most of their time burrowed into the ground, so they might be under the very sand you're walking on. Like other salamanders, they can survive being partially frozen in winter's cold temperatures.

OWL ◯ 3 POINTS

There are two owl species you're likely to see at this national park. The first is the burrowing owl, which lives in the ground and has long legs. The other is the northern pygmy-owl. It's small for an owl at only 7 inches, but don't let that fool you. This ferocious hunter often catches smaller songbirds to eat.

KANGAROO RAT ○ 2 POINTS

This little rodent is common in the desert and has adapted quite well to the conditions of living in a dry area. In fact, it can go its entire life without drinking water. It gets the water and moisture it needs from a diet of seeds.

The kangaroo rat spends a lot of its life underground, but you can often see them scurrying across the dunes. They have big hind legs and a pouch near their mouths for carrying seeds—both of these attributes help give it the kangaroo name.

ABERT'S SQUIRREL ○ 2 POINTS

Abert's squirrel is a tree squirrel with large ear tufts. Some people even call them scrabbits (mixing the name squirrel and rabbits) because of their rabbit-like ears. It lives in montane forests, which exist in the foothills of this national park.

PHLOX ○ 2 POINTS

You can find phlox flowers in a lot of different places, including backyards in many towns. The phlox you're likely to see at this national park is called alpine phlox. It grows low to the ground in summer, usually in shades of purple, pink, or white. They smell good, so if you see some growing on a hill, go see for yourself.

BLACK CANYON
OF THE GUNNISON
NATIONAL PARK

LOCATION Western Colorado
SIZE 32,000+ acres
FAMOUS FOR Deep canyon along
the Gunnison River
ESTABLISHED 1999

5 NUMBER OF ITEMS

POINTS POSSIBLE 11

THE BLACK CANYON OF THE GUNNISON became a national monument in 1933 and was finally designated a national park in 1999. It has an incredibly steep descent from the top to the bottom. In fact, it's so steep that certain parts of the canyon (called The Narrows) receive less than an hour of sunlight per day. If you like canyons and witnessing nature's beauty up close, then you will want to experience this park.

GUNNISON RIVER ○ 2 POINTS

This river drops an average of 43 feet per mile through this canyon. By comparison, the Colorado River drops about 7.5 feet per mile in the Grand Canyon. To see this for yourself, hike the Chasm View Nature Trail where the river drops as much as 240 feet per mile.

RIVER OTTER ○ 3 POINTS

Look for river otters along the Gunnison River while in this national park. They are actually part of the weasel family and are carnivores who eat fish, frogs, birds, turtles, and other animals. When young otters (called pups) are born, they typically stay with their mother in dens for several months before venturing out. Even then, they might stay with her for up to a year before they truly go out on their own.

EAGLE ○ 2 POINTS

There are two possible eagles to see at this national park—the bald eagle and the golden eagle, both of which you can find hanging out on the edge of the river looking for fish. They can look very similar, especially in flight. As the bald eagle gets older it develops the traditional white head, so that will help you be able to identify it more easily.

PINYON PINE ○ 2 POINTS

The pinyon pine is a common conifer at this national park. You'll find them in areas called pygmy forests, which are known as miniature forests to many. These forests tend to have trees that grow smaller and slower. The pinyon pine produces an edible nut that is a traditional food source in some American Indian cultures.

JUNIPER TREE ○ 2 POINTS

Junipers are another common tree in these pygmy forests. They are a popular tree to photograph because of the way they seem to twist and turn. These juniper berries are poisonous to humans, but they provide good food for birds and other animals.

MESA VERDE
NATIONAL PARK

LOCATION Southwest Colorado
SIZE 52,000+ acres
FAMOUS FOR Pueblo cliff dwellings
ESTABLISHED 1906

5 NUMBER OF ITEMS

POINTS POSSIBLE **13**

MESA VERDE OFFERS an incredible glimpse into the past of the Pueblo people, who lived in this area more than 700 years ago. One of this park's biggest draws is the cliff dwellings, which are some of the best-preserved sites of ancient people in the United States. The structures here hang over the cliffs and even form small villages. You will learn so much about the people who came before us by visiting this park.

- -

PORCUPINE ○ 3 POINTS

Porcupines are actually rodents with short legs that have coats of sharp spines (also known as quills). These quills are a defense mechanism for the animals. They will sometimes shake them to make noise as a warning to other animals to stay away. While there have been rumors that porcupines can throw their quills several feet, this is probably unlikely. They do detach easily, though, which tends to keep other animals away!

COYOTE
○ 2 POINTS

Look and listen for coyotes while you're at Mesa Verde. Most people think of coyotes as hunters, but they will also feed on plants and berries. These dog-like animals can make a lot of different sounds, including growling, barking, and their famous howling you're likely to hear at night.

COLLARED LIZARD ○ 3 POINTS

This medium-sized lizard grows up to 10 inches long. If you're able to look closely, you'll see that it has two black collars around its neck, which is where the name comes from. The best way to see this lizard is to look for it sunning itself on a rock while probably waiting for grasshoppers or other insects to eat.

BLACK-CHINNED HUMMINGBIRD ○ 3 POINTS

If you think you saw a dragonfly swooping by, take a closer look because it might be the black-chinned hummingbird. The males have beautiful purple throats. This fast-moving bird can reach speeds of up to 30 mph when flying. And they move their tongue to eat nectar at a rate of roughly 17 licks per second!

YUCCA ○ 2 POINTS

Yuccas are tough plants that can survive some of the harshest conditions. They often grow in hot, dry places and are easy to recognize with their spiky, sword-shaped leaves. Thanks to their deep roots, they can last a long time without water. Their flowers, which are often white, provide a good nectar source for birds, butterflies, and other insects.

SOUTHWEST

LESSER LONG-NOSED BAT

SAGUARO CACTUS

COLIMA WARBLER

COATI

WHITE SANDS NATIONAL PARK

LOCATION Southern New Mexico
SIZE 145,000+ acres
FAMOUS FOR Incredible sand dunes
ESTABLISHED 2019

5 NUMBER OF ITEMS

POINTS POSSIBLE **11**

THIS NATIONAL PARK is home to the world's largest gypsum sand dunefield. It's a rare kind of sand and is quite pale in color, so it almost seems like you're walking on snow! This area was established as a national monument in 1933, and finally earned the honor of being a national park in 2019. One of the most popular activities here among families is to go sledding! You bring a sled and then zoom down the big dune hill for a truly unique national park experience.

SAND ○ 1 POINT

You can't miss this pale, magical sand. It has unique qualities too. For instance, it doesn't absorb sun like typical sand, so you can always walk on it without burning your feet!

ORYX ○ 2 POINTS

Within this national park, you can find the African oryx. This large species of antelope (up to 450 pounds) was originally from eastern parts of Africa and was brought to the area in the 1960s and 1970s. Today they are considered to be an invasive animal that is damaging to the local ecosystem. The National Park Service strives to keep them out of the park, but you can still sometimes see them throughout the dunes.

FULL MOON ○ 3 POINTS

This one is all about timing your visit to White Sands during a full moon. It's common here to go on a midnight hike, which is especially magical during a full moon. Plan ahead to have this unique experience in the Southwest.

CHIHUAHUAN RAVEN
○ **3 POINTS**

This raven looks like a cross between an American crow and a common raven. It's incredibly experienced at surviving the harsh, hot conditions of the Southwest. It has a thick black bill and an impressive wingspan, reaching up to 43 inches wide!

AGAVE ○ **2 POINTS**

Look for an agave plant growing in the desert of this national park. They have stiff, succulent-type leaves. Many people think agaves are a type of cacti, but they're not. Many times, agaves will die after they flower, so if you do see one blooming, consider yourself lucky!

CARLSBAD CAVERNS
NATIONAL PARK

LOCATION Southeast New Mexico
SIZE 46,000+ acres
FAMOUS FOR More than 100
limestone caves
ESTABLISHED 1930

5 NUMBER OF ITEMS

POINTS POSSIBLE **10**

LOCATED IN THE GUADALUPE MOUNTAINS, this national park has more than 100 caves, including the most famous of them all, Carlsbad Cavern. This cave has a huge limestone chamber called the Big Room that is roughly 4,000 feet long, more than 600 feet wide, and more than 240 feet high. This makes it the largest cave chamber in North America. This park isn't just caves, though. It has many acres of protected wilderness, which helps the area's plants and wildlife.

BRAZILIAN FREE-TAILED BATS ○ 2 POINTS

Every night, more than 400,000 of these bats will emerge from the caves to feed during the night. It can be pretty spectacular to witness their impressive flights as they zip through the air. Each night, a single bat will eat at least 250 insects!

RINGTAIL ○ 3 POINTS

Ringtails are small mammals that are closely related to raccoons. They look like a cross between a cat and a raccoon, and visitors love them because they have a definite cute factor. They have excellent hearing, eyesight, and climbing skills. If you want to see one, ask a local ranger for tips.

CAVE CRICKET ○ 2 POINTS

As you go into the caves at this national park, pay attention to the animals you might see down below. You should be able to find many insects, including the cave cricket. They have long legs, including enormous hind legs. They might look intimidating, but they are harmless and a great thing to spot in the caves!

CARLSBAD CAVERN
◯ **2 POINTS**

Be sure to visit the big cave that gave this national park its name. This cave (as well as others in this park) formed millions of years ago when hydrogen-sulfide-rich water seeped through cracks and faults of the limestone in the area. This acid slowly dissolved the rocks to form the caves we know today.

WITCH'S FINGER
◯ **1 POINT**

If you go into Carlsbad Cavern, it would be hard to miss this popular sight. The Witch's Finger is a stalagmite (a rock formation growing up from the floor of a cave) within the cave. This is one of many that have names at the park. Ask a park ranger for tips on where to see others.

GUADALUPE
MOUNTAINS
NATIONAL PARK

LOCATION West Texas
SIZE 86,000+ acres
FAMOUS FOR Highest point in Texas
ESTABLISHED 1972

5 NUMBER OF ITEMS

POINTS POSSIBLE **11**

YOU'VE GOT MOUNTAINS, deserts, dunes, and canyons all in one spot when you visit this national park. Nearby are the Guadalupe Mountains, which include the highest point in Texas—Guadalupe Peak at 8,751 feet. This area is also known as the Capitan Reef, because it used to be entirely under the sea. However, millions of years ago, tectonic activity began to lift up the area and the mountains we see today. Because of this, it's considered to be one of the best-preserved Permian fossil reefs in the world.

JAVELINA ○ 2 POINTS
The javelina looks like a wild pig or wild hog, but it's actually a member of the peccary family. A native species in this area, they will often burrow away in caves or dens. Javelinas eat a mix of plants and other small desert animals like lizards.

ROADRUNNER ○ 3 POINTS
On cooler nights, roadrunners can lower their body temperature to conserve energy. This is considered a type of torpor. Then in the mornings, roadrunners will often hang out in the sun with their feathers out as a way to warm up again.

ALLIGATOR JUNIPER
◯ 2 POINTS

This juniper has a cool pattern once you get close to it. The bark's cracked scales look a lot like alligator skin. Junipers produce both seeds and berries, which feed area wildlife, making them an important plant in this area of the Southwest.

PHAINOPEPLA ◯ 2 POINTS

These Southwest birds have a distinct crest, much like a cardinal. Males are jet black while females are lighter and more gray overall. Growing about 8 inches tall, these birds look really beautiful in flight. They mostly eat berries, including mistletoe berries in winter.

FOSSIL ◯ 2 POINTS

A unique thing about this park is the way fossils have been preserved. This entire area used to be underwater, and because it's now exposed, you can easily spot a fossil while out and about on a hike.

BIG BEND
NATIONAL PARK

LOCATION West Texas
SIZE 801,000+ acres
FAMOUS FOR Rio Grande River
and the Chihuahuan Desert
ESTABLISHED 1944

6 NUMBER OF ITEMS

POINTS POSSIBLE **15**

BIG BEND, which is located near the Rio Grande and the Mexico border, is home to the Chisos Mountains, also known as the Chisos. This entire mountain range is located within this national park, including Emory Peak that sits at 7,825 feet tall. This park has an important job when it comes to conservation. More than 1,200 plants, 450 birds, 50 reptiles, and 75 mammals call this area home. There are incredible resources within the parks to help support all these nature treasures. It's also a beautiful, remote area to visit if you don't like a lot of traffic or crowds. Additionally, it's one of the best places in the country for stargazing. With dark night skies, you can see stars for miles and miles.

MEXICAN LONG-NOSED BAT ○ 3 POINTS
This rare bat has been considered endangered for many years, and Big Bend is one of the only—and best—places to see one for yourself. Considered a nectar-eating bat, it feeds on fruit, nectar, and pollen. Look for it roosting, as it's coming out at dusk, or near cacti flowers.

COLIMA WARBLER ○ 3 POINTS
Here's a warbler you won't find in any other parts of the United States. You pretty much need to be in Big Bend to see it. These birds tend to hide away in the mountains, always on the hunt for insects. Check with locals for tips on the best places to spot one.

BIG BEND SLIDER ○ 2 POINTS
This aquatic turtle (also called the Mexican Plateau slider) spends a lot of its life in or around the water. Look for one sunning on rocks near the water. They like muddy bottoms, often in ponds or rivers, where they can feed on growing vegetation.

BIG BEND BLUEBONNETS
◯ **2 POINTS**

Bluebonnets, which are the state flower of Texas, have deep blue blooms. Big Bend bluebonnets, *Lupinus havardii*, are a special variety that grow up to 3 feet tall, which is often taller than regular bluebonnets. Look for these joyful plants blooming in spring.

RIO GRANDE RIVER
◯ **2 POINTS**

The Rio Grande River forms part of the international border between the United States and Mexico, and more than 100 of those miles run through Big Bend. It's an important river for biodiversity as roughly 120 different fish species are found in these waters, including about 70 species not found anywhere else in the world.

MILKY WAY   ◯ **3 POINTS**

Big Bend is considered one of the best places in the country to see the Milky Way. Out of all the national parks in the Lower 48, it has the least amount of light pollution. This means on a really clear night, you'll be able to see thousands and thousands of stars, as far as the eye can see—which is what we know as the Milky Way.

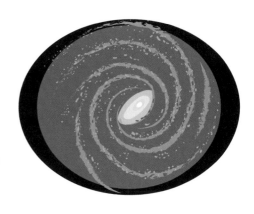

SAGUARO
NATIONAL PARK

LOCATION Near Tucson, Arizona
SIZE 91,000+ acres
FAMOUS FOR Saguaro cacti
ESTABLISHED 1994

5 NUMBER OF ITEMS

POINTS POSSIBLE **13**

TAKE A TRIP TO THE SONORAN DESERT and you will see incredible Southwestern treasures. This national park is home to more than 500 animal species and 2,000 plant species, including the signature saguaro cacti. Scientists estimate that there are more than 2 million of these cacti within the park borders. While you're here, be sure to check out the more than 165 miles of hiking trails. The park has two main districts: the Rincon Mountain District to the east of Tucson and the Tucson Mountain District further west.

LESSER LONG-NOSED BAT
○ **3 POINTS**

There are some pretty incredible bat species in the Southwest, including the lesser long-nosed bat. They will often feed on cacti flowers at night, which is when the blooms open up. They will roost in caves, often hundreds or thousands at a time.

COATI ○ **3 POINTS**

The coati (or white-nosed coati) is a member of the raccoon family and has a long snout. They are always on the move, foraging for nuts, berries, and plants. You can also see them flipping over rocks as they look for small lizards and snakes to eat.

GILA WOODPECKER ○ **2 POINTS**

Most woodpeckers depend on trees, but not the Gila. This southwestern woodpecker can survive just fine without any trees, even hollowing out saguaro cacti for a nesting spot. These birds have a distinct black-and-white pattern and long bills.

GILA MONSTER
○ 3 POINTS

The Gila monster is a venomous lizard in the Southwest that can grow up to 2 feet long. While it has a scary-sounding name, you shouldn't need to worry about it because it moves really slowly and mostly keeps away from humans.

SAGUARO CACTUS ○ 2 POINTS

The saguaro is the largest cactus in the United States. These incredible plants don't need a lot of water in order to survive. Most of their roots are less than 6 inches deep, but they have one tap root that extends down into the ground for more than 2 feet. This helps the plant conserve water and survive in the desert.

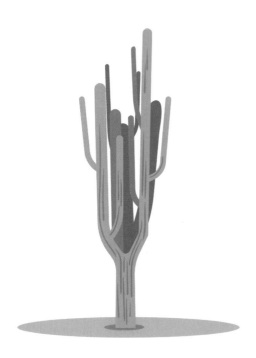

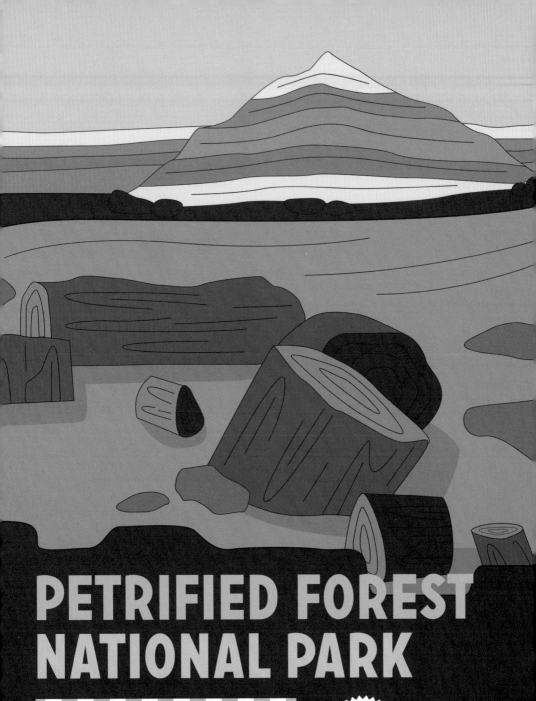

PETRIFIED FOREST NATIONAL PARK

LOCATION Eastern Arizona
SIZE 93,000+ acres
FAMOUS FOR World's largest
concentration of petrified wood
ESTABLISHED 1962

6 NUMBER OF ITEMS

POINTS POSSIBLE **14**

LOVE FOSSILS? Then put Petrified Forest National Park high on your list of places to visit. The entire area is well known for its fossils, most notably the fallen trees that are now petrified wood. These trees lived roughly 225 million years ago. This entire area is part of the Painted Desert, and many important plants and animals in this area benefit from conservation efforts of this and other national parks. In addition to fossils, you'll find badlands, buttes, and mesas.

- -

KIT FOX ○ 3 POINTS

This is the smallest fox you can find in North America, weighing only 5 pounds. Their large ears help them hear prey like mice under the ground so they can catch them. Kit foxes often live together and are considered endangered in most places.

BLACK-TAILED JACKRABBIT ○ 2 POINTS

The black-tailed jackrabbit can reach speeds of up to 40 mph, especially when it's trying to outrun a predator like a coyote. If it is being chased it will sometimes move in a zigzag shape to try to fool them and get away.

EVENING PRIMROSE
○ 2 POINTS

These beautiful flowers definitely live up to their name. Evening primrose opens in the late afternoon and closes up at sunrise. They often have white flowers in the wild, which have a lemony scent. This flower is popular with butterflies, hummingbirds, and other animals looking for nectar.

PAINTED DESERT ○ 2 POINTS
You're in the Painted Desert, so you should see it up close. When you find the Painted Desert Rim Trail in the park you'll soon understand why the desert gets this name. Look down, and you'll see that the beautiful layers of rock look as if they've been painted onto the landscape.

HORNED LARK ○ 3 POINTS
Horned larks are unique songbirds that have yellow faces with black masks—or rather, tiny little black tufts that look like horns on either side of their head. They like to hang out in big, open fields and will nest on the ground.

PETRIFIED WOOD ○ 2 POINTS
Petrified wood is essentially a tree or plant whose original trunk or stem has been replaced by stone due to a unique mineralization process. You can find plenty of places to see petrified wood in this national park. One of the best is called the Crystal Forest.

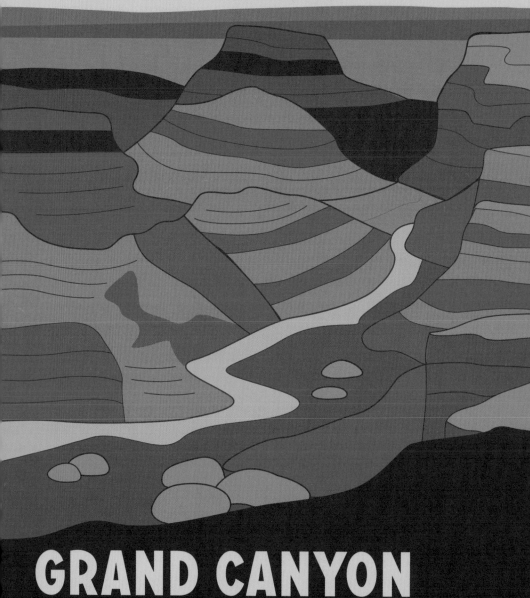

GRAND CANYON
NATIONAL PARK

LOCATION Northern Arizona
SIZE 1.2+ million acres
FAMOUS FOR Incredible canyon
and the Colorado River
ESTABLISHED 1919

10
NUMBER OF ITEMS

POINTS POSSIBLE
18

POPULAR GRAND CANYON National Park receives more than 6 million visitors every year. This area was quite remote until the railroad system was developed in the late 1800s. Then more and more people started coming to see this natural wonder for themselves. This included President Theodore Roosevelt who after visiting the site said, "The Grand Canyon fills me with awe. It is beyond comparison—beyond description." Many people feel similarly when they go to the Grand Canyon for the first time. You really do have to see it in person because its scale is hard to put into words.

- -

BIGHORN SHEEP ○ 2 POINTS

The bighorn sheep living in the Grand Canyon have adapted to extreme and rugged conditions over time. Look for them on steep sandstone cliffs—they can stand on ledges that are just 2 inches wide! If you see one, you'll probably see more since they like to travel in groups.

SQUIRREL ○ 1 POINT

You can see two different unique squirrels in the Grand Canyon—the Abert's squirrel and the Kaibab squirrel. Scientists used to think these were the same squirrel, but they've separated them. They both have ear tufts that make them look like they have long ears. Ask a park ranger to help you learn where to look for them.

TARANTULA ○ 3 POINTS

As you're hiking in the Grand Canyon, be sure to watch where you step because you might come across a tarantula in the wild. These hairy spiders grow up to 4 inches and create homes in burrows under the ground. Tarantulas have a venomous gland they can use on prey, but they are not poisonous to humans, so don't be afraid.

CALIFORNIA CONDOR
○ 3 POINTS

California condors have a wingspan of nearly 10 feet, which makes them the largest North American landbird. These sizeable birds nest in the park as well as in parts of Utah and California. For tips on where to see one, ask a park ranger.

COLORADO RIVER ○ 2 POINTS

The entire Colorado River runs 1,450 miles, starting in Rocky Mountain National Park and ending in the Gulf of California. Around 277 miles of the river flows through the Grand Canyon, but it's not always easy to see. You'll have to do some hiking to reach the mighty river yourself. Or book a float trip, which is an epic way to see the Grand Canyon.

WATCHTOWER ○ 2 POINTS

The Desert View Watchtower is an iconic 70-foot-high structure on the south rim of the canyon. Built in 1932 out of stone, it's now designated as a National Historical Landmark. It was designed to look like a Puebloan watchtower. You can climb the stairs to get one of the most incredible views in the area.

ELK ○ 2 POINTS

The Rocky Mountain elk is a common sight in the Grand Canyon, even walking around the roadways and visitor's center area. When male elk first get their antlers, they are covered in a velvety fuzz. But as the elk get older the fuzz disappears and the antlers harden.

MULE ○ 1 POINT

If you're anywhere near the trails, there's a good chance you'll come across a mule. These animals are trained to take regular trips down the canyon and back. They've been getting people and supplies in and out of this area for more than 100 years and are important to the local economy.

TRAILHEAD ○ 1 POINT

Even if you don't do a big hike in and out of the Grand Canyon, at least take the time to find one of the famous trailheads. This is a great place for people watching as you see people setting out or coming back from a tough hike.

TRAIN ○ 1 POINT

The Grand Canyon Railway was completed in 1901, and it was a big success in helping get tourists into the park. For a while, this railway was out of service, but it's operating once again thanks to restoration efforts.

UTAH AND NEVADA

LEHMAN CAVES

UINTA CHIPMUNK

GRAY FOX

WESTERN KINGBIRD

BRISTLECONE PINE

WESTERN COLLARED LIZARD

ARCHES
NATIONAL PARK

LOCATION Southeast Utah
SIZE 76,000+ acres
FAMOUS FOR Large concentration of arches
ESTABLISHED 1929

6 NUMBER OF ITEMS

POINTS POSSIBLE **12**

ARCHES IS ONE OF THE MOST ICONIC signs of our National Park System with its famous Delicate Arch regularly showing up in art, pictures, and even on the Utah license plate. The park has more than 2,000 natural stone arches, which is the highest density of arches in the world! It's a popular park, receiving more than 1.5 million visitors each year. Whether you plan to drive through this park to see the sights or stop to hike a few miles to some of the epic, hidden arches, there's never a bad time to go. Just keep in mind it's a high desert area with less than 10 inches of rainfall a year, so plan ahead and bring your water!

- -

MULE DEER
◯ **2 POINTS**

These deer got their name because they look like they have mule ears. They've adapted really well to all sorts of conditions, including the rocky desert of Arches. They often live 9 to 11 years in the wild on their own.

WESTERN COLLARED LIZARD ◯ **3 POINTS**

You can recognize this lizard by the two black rings around its neck. While some lizards will easily lose their tails and grow them back, this one has a tougher tail. It doesn't usually lose it, but if it does, it won't grow back. These lizards are often on the move, looking to eat bugs and even other lizards.

WESTERN SCRUB-JAY
○ 2 POINTS

The western scrub-jay has bright blue outer feathers and a gray underside. This jay is a pretty fearless and loud bird, even stopping at picnic areas to see if it can steal any food. They typically eat insects, fruit, and seeds. They've even been seen sitting on mule deer, picking and eating insects off them.

DELICATE ARCH ○ 2 POINTS

Delicate Arch is 52 feet tall and incredibly popular among visitors. This arch and others in the park get their red coloring from iron oxide. It's a challenging hike (3 miles roundtrip) to see the arch up close. For the 2002 Olympics, the Olympic torch was carried under the arch on its way to Salt Lake City.

SUNSET ◯ 1 POINT

Delicate Arch is one great spot in the park to catch the sunset—
with the sun behind it, it's the perfect setting for some pretty epic
photos—but there are many others as well. As you plan your visit,
talk to a park ranger about lesser-known spots. Be sure to arrive
early, then set yourself up for a sunset picture.

BALANCED ROCK ◯ 2 POINTS

Balanced Rock is another popular sight in Arches. It really looks
like it's perfectly balancing on top of a tall structure, about to
topple. It's a short hike to get up close to, and it makes for a really
cool photo.

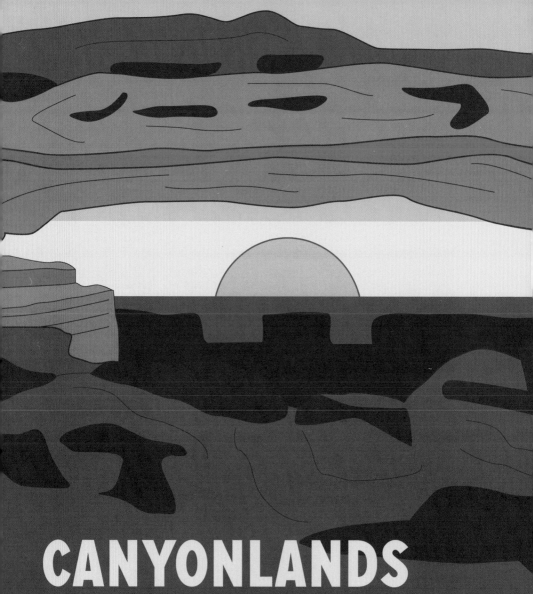

CANYONLANDS
NATIONAL PARK

LOCATION Southeast Utah
SIZE 337,000+ acres
FAMOUS FOR Canyons around the
Colorado and Green Rivers
ESTABLISHED 1964

6 NUMBER OF ITEMS

POINTS POSSIBLE **13**

THIS IS THE LARGEST national park in Utah—but it's also the least visited. Don't overlook it, though. This park's incredible diversity includes canyons, mesas, buttes, and arches. Much of the land has been carved by the Colorado and Green Rivers. Both are still important to conservation efforts in this area today. While this national park is a bit off the beaten path, it's well worth the detour. The famous author Edward Abbey once described it as "the most weird, wonderful, magical place on earth—there is nothing else like it anywhere."

BOBCAT ○ 3 POINTS

Bobcats have up to six babies (called kittens) in one litter. They keep them inside their dens for a couple of months, and then they slowly start bringing them out to teach them how to hunt. They continue to learn for many months until they go out on their own around the 1 year mark.

WHITE-TAILED ANTELOPE SQUIRREL
○ 2 POINTS

These little ground squirrels look a bit like chipmunks. They have two white stripes running from their shoulders through their hind. They tend to avoid the really hot part of the day, instead coming out in the early evening. When they're not out and about, they stay underground in their burrows.

MESA ARCH
○ 2 POINTS

This arch is one of the most popular areas of the park because it's easy to get to and offers beautiful photo opportunities. The arch is 27 feet long and perfectly frames the canyon below. Sunrise is a perfect time to visit this iconic arch.

GREEN RIVER ○ 2 POINTS

The Green River has a slight green coloring because of the sediments within it. The entire river is 730 miles long with about 450 of those miles being in Utah. This river meets the Colorado River in Canyonlands National Park.

PINYON JAY
○ **2 POINTS**

The pinyon jay is a member of the jay family, but it doesn't have a crest like other jays. It is light blue overall with a dagger-like bill. They often travel through trees in groups as they look for seeds.

SHAFER TRAIL ○ **2 POINTS**

This incredibly steep, iconic backcountry road winds 1,500 feet from the top of the canyon to the bottom. Not all cars are equipped to handle the unpaved drive down, but it's still worth seeing the beautiful scene for yourself, even just by standing at the top of the canyon. You'll get a great view of the river, too.

CAPITOL REEF
NATIONAL PARK

LOCATION Southern Utah
SIZE 241,000+ acres
FAMOUS FOR Red and rugged landscape
ESTABLISHED 1971

5 NUMBER OF ITEMS

POINTS POSSIBLE **11**

THIS NATIONAL PARK is part of a special area called the Waterpocket Fold. This is essentially a 100-mile fold in the Earth's crust, which gives you a unique and beautiful look at the layers and layers of rock. Since "reef" refers to a ridge of rock or sand, either in the ocean or on land, it's a fitting part of the park's name. The first part of the name, Capitol, is a reference to the dome of the United States Capitol Building in Washington, D.C. This area is an important part of the Southwest, helping to preserve land for area plants and animals.

- -

GOLDEN EAGLE
◯ **3 POINTS**

Only three different raptors have feathers down their legs and all the way to their toes: the rough-legged hawk, the ferruginous hawk, and the golden eagle. The golden eagle is found around the world and is a national symbol to Albania, Austria, Germany, Kazakhstan, and Mexico.

CANYON TREEFROG
◯ **2 POINTS**

The canyon treefrog is typically gray or brown in color. They quickly and easily blend into their surroundings—you might be looking directly at one and still not see it! These big insect eaters are always looking for their next meal.

SIDE-BLOTCHED LIZARD ○ 2 POINTS

These lizards grow about 6 inches long, including the tail, and are some of the most common lizard species in the Southwest. They can change color from one season to the next, and males often have bright throats.

FRUIT TREES ○ 2 POINTS

Have you ever heard of a national park with its own orchard? Capitol Reef has one, thanks to many years of care and preservation. When the fruit trees in this national park are ripe, you are invited to stop by the orchard and pick your own! Even if nothing is available for picking at the moment, it's still worth seeing the fruit trees for yourself.

PANORAMA POINT ○ 2 POINTS

This viewpoint is easy to access off the highway and offers some of the best scenes in the area. It's particularly popular at sunset, and it continues to draw visitors at night as well. It's a great place to view the stars!

BRYCE CANYON
NATIONAL PARK

LOCATION Southern Utah
SIZE 35,000+ acres
FAMOUS FOR Hoodoo formations
ESTABLISHED 1928

5 NUMBER OF ITEMS

POINTS POSSIBLE **9**

GO TO BRYCE CANYON BEFORE SUNRISE, and when the sun peeks up over the horizon, you'll experience one of the most unique scenes of the Southwest. Though this national park is a bit of a detour for most, it's worth the trip to see the world's largest collection of hoodoos. What are hoodoos exactly? These are geological structures that have formed over the years by frost weathering and stream erosion. The many colors and layers of these rocks make for an incredible view, especially when you're standing on the edge of the namesake Bryce Canyon—which is actually not a canyon at all but a giant natural amphitheater. In addition to this main attraction, the national park has an 18-mile road, popular for those who want to see it all. You'll find many opportunities for camping, hiking, and exploring along the way.

UTAH PRAIRIE DOG ◯ 2 POINTS

In the northern parts of Bryce Canyon where there are meadows, you'll find the Utah prairie dog. They live in burrows together, hanging out in what's called towns. It's common to see them perched on their hind legs, keeping an eye out on the world around them.

UINTA CHIPMUNK ◯ 2 POINTS

This medium-sized chipmunk (up to 9 inches) also goes by the name hidden forest chipmunk. They like being tucked away in conifer forests of pine, fir, and spruce trees. After spending most of the winter in their dens, they are often on the move during spring and summer.

WESTERN KINGBIRD ○ 2 POINTS

Keep an eye out for this small gray bird with a yellow belly in all parts of this national park. As a member of the flycatcher family, you'll often see it perched on a wire or brand, waiting to swoop down to catch a fly or another insect. They will also eat berries and fruit in the wild.

BRYCE AMPHITHEATER
○ 2 POINTS

No visit to Bryce Canyon is complete without a stop at the famous amphitheater, which is home to the many hoodoos. Stop at one of the popular viewpoints like Bryce Point, Inspiration Point, Sunrise Point, and Sunset Point to see the many great angles of this park.

HOODOO ○ 1 POINT

Hoodoos are created within sedimentary rock. This former plateau has been subjected to extremes of weather for centuries. As water seeps down into fissures in the rock then freezes at night and expands, it breaks away "wedges" of the rock from the inside out until it forms the shapes you see today. They often have beautiful, colorful patterns, and they can be anywhere from 5 to 150 feet tall. Many people say the shapes remind them of totem poles.

ZION
NATIONAL PARK

LOCATION Southwest Utah
SIZE 146,000+ acres
FAMOUS FOR Stunning sandstone
and canyons
ESTABLISHED 1919

7 NUMBER OF ITEMS

POINTS POSSIBLE **16**

ZION MAY TAKE YOUR BREATH AWAY as you drive into the park for the first time. Less than 3 hours from Vegas, Zion is a popular destination and is regularly in the top five list of most visited national parks. The canyon running through Zion is 2,000 feet deep and millions of years in the making. Each year, people come here for epic hikes like The Narrows and Angels Landing. With such a popular park, be prepared to show up early or catch the shuttle buses to get to some of the most popular destinations. If you're looking for a taste of the Southwest mixed with a bit of adventure, then this park will quickly become a favorite.

- -

MEXICAN SPOTTED OWL
○ **3 POINTS**

This is one of the largest owls in North America with a wingspan of nearly 45 inches. They have dark eyes and white spots all over. They can be challenging to spot in the wild because they remain well hidden, so try listening for their hooting instead.

FOX ○ **3 POINTS**

It's the gray fox you'll be looking for in Zion. This small but mighty fox is a great hunter, chasing down smaller mammals or even reptiles like lizards. They are excellent climbers, so if you're trying to spot one, don't forget to look up. It might be hiding in the treetops.

LIZARD ◯ 2 POINTS

You can find several species of lizards throughout Zion. This includes the common plateau lizard (which has patches of blue along its belly) and the Great Basin collared lizard (which has been known to stand up and run on its hind legs).

OBSERVATION POINT ◯ 3 POINTS

This is one of the most challenging but amazing trails in Zion. You'll climb 2,300 feet on this 8-mile roundtrip hike to get to an amazing view at the end. If you choose to take it on, pack plenty of water and snacks. And don't forget to capture pictures!

COURT OF THE PATRIARCHS ◯ 2 POINTS

This is a group of sandstone cliffs in Zion, and it's a much easier viewpoint to get to, compared to many others in the park. The mountain is named after the biblical figures of Abraham, Isaac, and Jacob. It's considered the shortest trail at Zion, only taking a couple of minutes!

VIRGIN RIVER ◯ 1 POINT

Much of the beautiful scenery you see in this area has been carved by the Virgin River over millions of years. The entire river is 162 miles long, and it was officially Utah's first wild and scenic river, which was dedicated in 2009.

THE NARROWS
◯ 2 POINTS

The narrowest part of the canyons within Zion National Park is an epic, popular hike. If you choose to hike through The Narrows, be prepared to get wet as you wade through the Virgin River. The smallest opening in The Narrows is only 20 to 30 feet wide.

GREAT BASIN
NATIONAL PARK

LOCATION Eastern Nevada
SIZE 77,000+ acres
FAMOUS FOR Basin formations
throughout the area
ESTABLISHED 1986

5
NUMBER OF ITEMS

POINTS POSSIBLE
11

THIS PARK'S NAME COMES directly from the Great Basin—a dry, mountainous region between the Sierra Nevada and Wasatch Mountains. The groves of bristlecone pines are a unique feature of this park. It also has epic caves, great hiking, and lots of interesting plants and animals to discover. There's a saying around here that goes like this: "Half the park is after dark." This means get ready for some spectacular stargazing after the sun has set for the day!

BRISTLECONE PINE
○ 2 POINTS

This pine has a reputation for being the oldest non-clonal species on the planet, which means the trunk of the tree is as old as the root system. These trees are incredibly tough, surviving challenging conditions for thousands of years. Because of the high winds these trees have dealt with over the years, they are often twisted into unique shapes.

PYGMY RABBIT
○ 3 POINTS

The pygmy rabbit is the smallest North American rabbit at less than 1 foot tall. You can often find this rabbit in areas with sagebrush. They dig their own burrows, which other animals will try to use and take over as well.

WHEELER PEAK ◯ 2 POINTS

Taking Wheeler Peak Scenic Drive is a popular activity in this national park. It leads you to the highest point in the park and also the second highest point in Nevada at 13,065 feet. The winding road is slow going, but the end result is beautiful as you look out over the Great Basin Desert.

LEHMAN CAVES ◯ 2 POINTS

After you experience the tall peaks of this national park, go underground to see the impressive caves. These limestone caves are home to rare shield formations. Cave tours are popular, so book early!

STARS ◯ 2 POINTS

This is going to be an easy one to check off the list. The stars at this national park are truly incredible because this is where you'll find some of the darkest skies in the entire United States. If you really love stars, check out the annual astronomy festival.

CALIFORNIA

CALIFORNIA POPPY

WHITE-HEADED WOODPECKER

BADGER

CACTUS WREN

BOBCAT

EL CAPITAN

REDWOOD
NATIONAL PARK

LOCATION **Northern California**
SIZE **112,000+ acres**
FAMOUS FOR **Redwood trees**
ESTABLISHED **1968**

6 NUMBER OF ITEMS

POINTS POSSIBLE **12**

REDWOOD NATIONAL PARK protects some of the tallest trees in the world. During the 1800s and early 1900s, logging negatively impacted the more than 2 million acres of forests in this area. Then in the 1920s, conservation efforts began to protect both the redwoods and surrounding land. Today, those efforts have gone a long way toward keeping the redwoods thriving, which, in turn, has led to helping other area plants, trees, and animals survive.

- -

ROOSEVELT ELK
 **2 POINTS**

Roosevelt elk were named after President Theodore Roosevelt. These beautiful mammals typically have just one baby (called a calf) each year. The little ones will start standing within an hour of being born, and then they'll stay with their mom until the next spring when the birthing cycle starts over again.

CALIFORNIA SEA LION
○ **3 POINTS**

It's easy to understand why "lion" is in their name when you hear these animals roar loudly. Just a few days after a sea lion baby (or pup) is born, the mom will leave them in a group with other sea lions and young so she can go out to sea to fish. When she gets back, she knows which baby is hers by smelling it. Look for sea lions along the coasts of this national park.

BANANA SLUG ○ 2 POINTS

Banana slugs are huge, reaching up to 10 inches. They are common throughout the Pacific Northwest and are easily recognizable by their yellow color and their slime. You might think they'd be easy to see, but they blend into the background really well. They can also adjust their coloring based on their current environment. So you'll have to look extra close to find a banana slug.

REDWOOD TREE ○ 1 POINT

If you want to see a tree as old as a dinosaur, this is the one. Well, almost—records show that redwood trees showed up on Earth just after the dinosaurs. This means they've been around for about 240 million years. The oldest redwoods that are still growing today are around 2,000 years old and available to see right in this national park.

ANNA'S HUMMINGBIRD
○ 2 POINTS

This is one of the few hummingbird species that will fly this far north up the West Coast. It's a tiny bird that builds a nest about the size of a walnut, but it packs an incredible punch. It beats its wings up to 50 times per second and regularly moves at speeds of 25 mph or more.

FERN ○ 2 POINTS

Fern Canyon is a magical place near Redwood National Park. It's technically in the state park, but the land is managed in partnership with the National Park Service. It's home to ancient ferns that seem to grow up, down, and all around. This place has even been used in filming for dinosaur movies. You'll want to see this beautiful spot for yourself and get some pictures while you're at it.

LASSEN
NATIONAL PARK

LOCATION Northeast California
SIZE 106,000+ acres
FAMOUS FOR Largest plug dome volcano in the world
ESTABLISHED 1916

6
NUMBER OF ITEMS

POINTS POSSIBLE
15

THIS UNIQUE NATIONAL PARK is one of the few areas in the world where you can find all four types of volcanoes—plug dome, shield, cinder cone, and stratovolcano. It's also home to Lassen Peak, the largest plug dome volcano in the world. Yes, there's a lot of hydrothermal activity going on here, but it also has lakes, meadows, wildflowers, and more. It's a must-see national park when you're in this area.

RED FOX
○ **3 POINTS**

Have you ever heard of the term vixen? This is what red fox females are called. Another cool fact about these mammals is that they have different numbers of toes. For example, five toes on their front paws and only four toes on their back paws. Red foxes aren't always easy animals to see, but keep an eye out especially early in the morning and at dusk.

GOLDEN-MANTLED GROUND SQUIRREL ○ 2 POINTS
Is it a chipmunk or a squirrel? It could pass for either! But this is a ground squirrel, which actually spends a lot of time underground. Whenever it's cold, they burrow. This is where they store their seeds and nuts, too.

WHITE-HEADED WOODPECKER ○ 2 POINTS
If there are pine trees around, especially ponderosa or sugar pines, keep an eye out for the white-headed woodpecker. It will hammer apart pine seeds to get at the meat. This Western bird has a distinct white head. The birds will often use drumming as a way to communicate with one another.

CALIFORNIA TORTOISESHELL BUTTERFLY ◯ 3 POINTS

This butterfly has bright orange wings, but that doesn't mean it's easy to see. When they perch and close up their wings, they actually look a lot like a dead leaf. Try to spot them flying through the flowers of this national park and notice their wings both open and closed.

PACIFIC TREEFROG ◯ 3 POINTS

The Pacific treefrog isn't very big at only 2 inches, but the flap on their neck can stretch ever bigger when they are calling. You might not see them very easily, but hearing them counts too. Try to spot them by looking for their light green shades, likely hanging out in a tree!

STEAM ◯ 2 POINTS

Some people think Lassen Volcanic National Park has geysers because of something called a terminal geyser. However, it's not really a geyser at all. It gives off this appearance, but it's actually a cold stream flowing over a steam vent. It's still a unique sight, so put it on your list for this park.

YOSEMITE
NATIONAL PARK

LOCATION Eastern California
SIZE 760,000+ acres
FAMOUS FOR Beautiful rock and
waterfall landscapes
ESTABLISHED 1890

10 NUMBER OF ITEMS

POINTS POSSIBLE **17**

YOU COULD SPEND DAYS IN YOSEMITE National Park and still not see it all. Between the giant sequoias and waterfalls to exploring incredible sights like Half Dome, it's easy to see why this national park is one of the most popular. Naturalist John Muir once wrote Yosemite "is by far the grandest of all the special temples of Nature I was ever permitted to enter." Even though this land was the third official national park, established in 1890, it actually received protection in 1864 when the Yosemite Land Grant was established–the first time anyone ever put forth action to protect public land in this way.

BLACK BEAR
○ **3 POINTS**

Did you know black bears are expert climbers? Even though they can weigh hundreds of pounds, they move really well up and down a tree, thanks to their strong claws. They can also move up to 35 mph, which can help them get a running start to scale a tree quickly, too. Experts say as many as 500 black bears live in Yosemite.

CALIFORNIA GROUND
SQUIRREL ○ **1 POINT**

These ground squirrels spend a lot of their lives underground where they store food, raise their young, and stay protected from predators. They'll often live in groups, though each family might have their own entrance to the burrow. Try to see if you can spot where this squirrel pops in and out of the ground.

STELLER'S JAY ◯ 2 POINTS

North America's largest jay (around 13 inches long) is a bright blue and black bird. They are big, loud, and common in the West. They will eat insects, seeds, nuts, other eggs, and even small animals. And watch out—they will also steal food from campsites and picnic areas!

YOSEMITE TOAD ◯ 2 POINT

If you want to see the Yosemite toad, then you'll have to be in California. This native toad loves high-elevation areas, where females will lay nearly 2,000 eggs; a small portion of these will hatch less than a week later. The population has been on the decline over the years, but it's worth looking for one.

HALF DOME ◯ 1 POINT

Half Dome might be the most recognizable rock formation in the world. Over the years, there has been a lot of speculation as to whether the other "half" of this rock eroded away or if it even existed at all. It sits nearly 9,000 feet in the air and is one of the most challenging hikes at this national park. It's not easy, but if you do choose to climb it, know you'll be hiking about 17 miles total.

SIERRA GARTER SNAKE ◯ 2 POINTS

Also known as Couch's garter snake, this non-poisonous snake often hangs out near or in the water. These snakes will eat toads, frogs, fish, and larvae they find in the water. They are a favorite among naturalists and are fun to look for while visiting the park.

SEQUOIA TREE ○ 2 POINTS

If you want to see sequoia trees in Yosemite National Park, it is possible in the Mariposa Grove. It's here where you'll find the trees with the thickest bark in the world. Two cool facts about sequoias is that they are naturally disease resistant, and they can also survive (and even thrive after) moderate forest fires.

EL CAPITAN ○ 1 POINT

El Capitan stands roughly 7,500 feet tall, which is about three times the height of the Eiffel Tower. It is known for being the tallest exposed vertical face of granite on Earth. This has attracted elite rock climbers from all over the world.

WATERFALL ○ 1 POINT

Yosemite is a popular destination for those who love to go chasing waterfalls. Between Yosemite Falls, at nearly 2,500 feet, to Vernal Falls, there are plenty of opportunities to see waterfalls here. All in all, there are about 25 waterfalls throughout the park, and many are easy to reach with a short hike.

CALIFORNIA POPPY ○ 2 POINTS

The California poppy became the state flower of California in 1903, and it's still an iconic sight today. You can see this flower throughout much of the state, including in Yosemite National Park. Look for the bright orange blooms in spring and summer. They often self-seed, meaning they easily spread on their own from one season to the next.

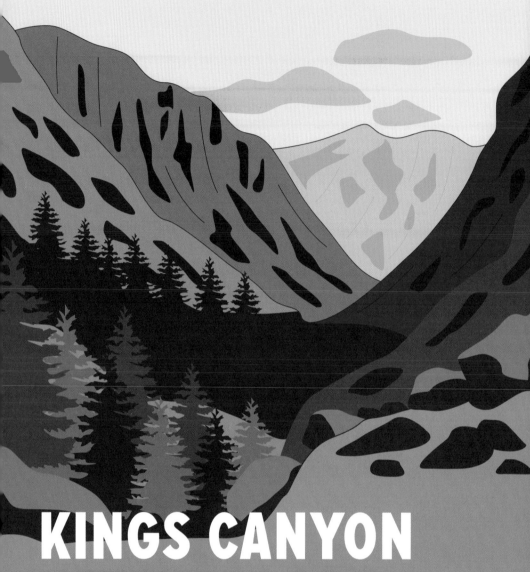

KINGS CANYON
NATIONAL PARK

LOCATION Eastern California
SIZE 461,000+ acres
FAMOUS FOR General Grant tree
ESTABLISHED 1940

5 NUMBER OF ITEMS

POINTS POSSIBLE **8**

DON'T OVERLOOK KINGS CANYON.

This national park doesn't get as much attention as Sequoia, but it's just as beautiful. Many people love it more because it's off the beaten path and has less traffic. This park is home to the largest remaining grove of sequoia trees in the world, so if big trees are what you're after, you definitely need to pay a visit. The naturalist John Muir even called it a "rival to Yosemite"!

GENERAL GRANT ○ 1 POINT

This giant sequoia is the second largest tree in the world at 267 feet tall and roughly 29 feet wide at the base. This means it's about as tall as a 16-story building. These trees are massive, and they weigh a lot, too. If you were to weigh General Grant, it would measure in at more than 1,200 tons!

WATERFALL
○ 1 POINT

Big trees and waterfalls go nicely together. You'll find several waterfalls in Kings Canyon, and most are very short hikes to view. Look for Grizzly Falls just outside the national park or Roaring Rivers Falls, which is especially strong in spring.

GOLDFINCH ○ 2 POINTS

You're likely to see the American goldfinch and the lesser goldfinch in this national park. Both are bright yellow, especially in spring and summer. They feed almost exclusively on seeds, so they're always on the move looking for food.

MOUNTAIN ○ 1 POINT

This should be an easy one to check off the list because the park has mountain views throughout. The Sierra Nevada mountain range runs more than 400 miles from north to south and another 70 miles across (east to west). The famous gold rush occurred at the foothills of these mountains, so it's steeped in California history.

BOBCAT
○ 3 POINTS

The bobcat, which is closely related to the lynx, is the most common wildcat in North America. In the wild this cat can look a lot like a dog or a big domestic cat. Don't let their smaller size fool you. They are fierce hunters, tracking down animals like squirrels, rabbits, and even bigger prey like deer.

SEQUOIA
NATIONAL PARK

LOCATION Eastern California
SIZE 404,000+ acres
FAMOUS FOR General Sherman tree
ESTABLISHED 1890

5 NUMBER OF ITEMS

POINTS POSSIBLE **11**

SEQUOIA NATIONAL PARK is home to many tall and famous attractions! Every year, roughly 1 million people pass through the park to see the famous giant sequoias. Here in the park's Giant Forest, you can find the General Sherman tree, which is the largest tree by volume on Earth. This same forest has 5 of the 10 largest trees in the world. In addition, this national park is home to Mount Whitney, the tallest point in the Lower 48 at 14,505 feet.

- - - - - - - - - - - - - - - - -

GENERAL SHERMAN
○ 2 POINTS

General Sherman is the world's largest tree when measured by volume. It stands 275 feet tall and is more than 36 feet wide at the base. The hike to see this tree is less than a mile, so it's worth putting on your list. It makes a great photo opportunity!

CALIFORNIA NEWT
○ 3 POINTS

The California newt is the largest native salamander species in this area, and they have distinct orange bellies. The adults can be really toxic, carrying the same amount of poison as a pufferfish, so it's best to leave this gorgeous, unique amphibian alone if you find it in the wild.

GENERAL SHERMAN

MOUNT WHITNEY ◯ 1 POINT

Standing at 14,505 feet, this is the largest mountain in the Lower 48 and one of the most popular mountains to climb in North America. Whenever people climb a mountain, they often have to acclimate to the change in elevation, meaning they have to get their body used to ascending several thousand feet in a single day. Around 30,000 people try to climb this mountain every year.

NUTHATCH
◯ 2 POINTS

You should be able to spot both the red-breasted and white-breasted nuthatch in this national park. Both birds have a unique habit of moving up a tree as if they're upside down. In fact, this behavior is a good way to know you're looking at a nuthatch. They move this way because they're searching for insects between the bark of trees.

BADGER ◯ 3 POINTS

If seeing wildlife is important to you, then put the badger on your list while you're at Sequoia. It's not going to be easy, but it's an awesome challenge. These little mammals are incredibly strong and use their claws to dig elaborate tunnels and burrows. They will often use these dens to store their food for later.

DEATH VALLEY
NATIONAL PARK

LOCATION Along the California–
Nevada border
SIZE 3.3 million+ acres
FAMOUS FOR The lowest point
in the United States
ESTABLISHED 1994

6
NUMBER OF ITEMS

POINTS POSSIBLE
13

IF YOU LIKE EXTREMES, then Death Valley should be on your list of places to experience. This area in the Mojave Desert is one of the hottest places on Earth. It's also home to Badwater Basin, the lowest point in North America at 282 feet below sea level. This is pretty amazing when you think about it because it's less than 100 miles away from the highest point in the lower 48 states, Mount Whitney. It can be dangerous to travel through Death Valley, so make sure you're prepared and have lots of water.

BLACK-TAILED JACKRABBIT ○ 2 POINTS

If you've never seen a jackrabbit before, then get ready to do a double take. The black-tailed jackrabbit (also called a desert hare) has ears that seem to defy gravity, standing up to 6 inches tall. These hares can reach speeds of up to 30 mph. They can also jump up to 20 feet in the air in an attempt to evade predators.

BIGHORN SHEEP ○ 3 POINTS

Bighorn sheep like to travel in groups. Most commonly, they'll gather in groups of 10 or so, but in some areas, their groups number more than 100! Young sheep will nurse with their mothers for several months, and then stay with them for another 2 to 3 years. Female sheep may stay with their mothers their whole lives while males will eventually leave to join another male-led group.

GREATER ROADRUNNER ○ 2 POINTS

Roadrunners are tough birds that can hold their own, no matter what habitat they're living in. They've been known to ➡

even take on and kill rattlesnakes! They can reach speeds of up to 15 mph, which is enough to outrun most prey. This makes up for their flying, which they aren't great at.

DESERT TORTOISE
○ 3 POINT

The desert tortoise reaches up to 15 inches long and up to 15 pounds. They are listed as threatened, and Death Valley is among the few places in the United States where you can see one. They often like spending time in their burrows, which they dig with their legs. In the wild, tortoises often live 30 to 50 years. Some have even been known to live more than 80 years!

BLACK MOUNTAINS
○ 1 POINT

You might not think of Death Valley as having mountains, but you can see some while at this national park. The Black Mountains reach heights of just over 6,000 feet above sea level. If you are up for about an 8-mile excursion check out the hike to Funeral Peak.

BADWATER BASIN ○ 2 POINTS

If you want to check out the lowest point in the country, this is it! Badwater Basin is 282 feet below sea level. Legend has it that the name came from a mule who was traveling in this area but wouldn't drink from the water because it was bad. The water here is very salty.

PINNACLES
NATIONAL PARK

LOCATION Central California
SIZE 26,600+ acres
FAMOUS FOR Large black
and gold pinnacles
ESTABLISHED 2013

6 NUMBER OF ITEMS

POINTS POSSIBLE **14**

PINNACLES IS ANOTHER NATIONAL PARK that often gets overlooked in favor of more famous parks, but it's a gorgeous place to visit near the Pacific coast. It has awe-inspiring rock formations, which attract thousands of rock climbers every year. There's really not a bad time to visit Pinnacles because every season offers something interesting. You should definitely have this newish national park on your list.

BLACK-TAILED DEER ○ 2 POINTS

You should be able to spot black-tailed deer throughout this national park, especially in the early morning and early evening when they are most active. During summer, these deer tend to go to higher elevations and then come back down in winter. Look for them in forests or near streams of water.

ACORN WOODPECKER
○ 2 POINTS

The acorn woodpecker lives up to its name by storing thousands of acorns in trees each year, sometimes working nonstop to build its collection. This species has a distinct look with red on the back of its head and markings that look like a mask. Acorn woodpecker young will sometimes stay with their parents for years to help raise and take care of new young.

CALIFORNIA CONDOR ○ 3 POINTS

California condors are part of the vulture family, and they're the largest bird in North America. These birds became extinct in the wild during the 1980s; since then, conservation efforts have been working to reintroduce them. The active efforts at Pinnacles to help increase the condors' population have been working. Keep an eye out for these majestic birds while you're there.

ROCK CLIMBER ○ 2 POINTS

Pinnacles is a popular national park for rock climbers, so you should be able to spot someone when you're out exploring. There are also plenty of places in the area where you can take lessons or rent equipment to try this sport for yourself.

ACMON BLUE BUTTERFLY
○ 3 POINTS

This West Coast butterfly is especially common in California. It's not very big–the wingspan is only about an inch. When it has its wings out, you can see the beautiful blue shades on top. But if it's perched with its wings closed, they look dull white with black spots. This means you'll have to pay attention if you want to see it!

CAVE ○ 2 POINTS

Pinnacles is home to two different caves: Balconies Cave and Bear Gulch Cave. A lot of caves in California were made from lava flows, but both of these were created because of cave-ins. Check at the visitor's center whether the caves are open to visitors and how to get there. If you do go inside the caves, be sure to keep an eye out for bats as well. This national park is home to 14 different bat species, and they'll definitely be hanging out in caves.

CHANNEL ISLANDS
NATIONAL PARK

LOCATION Off the coast of
Southern California
SIZE 249,000+ acres
FAMOUS FOR Lush natural islands
and marine life
ESTABLISHED 1980

5 NUMBER OF ITEMS

POINTS POSSIBLE **11**

CHANNEL ISLANDS NATIONAL PARK gives you that tropical experience without leaving the United States. This park is made up of five islands off the coast of California—San Miguel, Santa Rosa, Santa Cruz, Anacapa, and Santa Barbara. It's been a long journey to protect this public land. It started as a national monument in 1938, became a biosphere reserve in 1976, and finally earned its designation as a national park in 1980. It's an excellent place to experience beach life, go diving, or just soak up the sun.

ISLAND FOX ○ 3 POINTS

The island fox is unique to California. At roughly 12 inches high and only 4 to 5 pounds, it's about the size of many house cats (or roughly a third of the size of a gray fox). Their diet ranges from beetles and other bugs to mice, cactus, fruits, and even shellfish like crabs. The island fox has been considered threatened for many years, but they've been making a comeback thanks to conservation efforts.

ISLAND DEER MOUSE
○ 2 POINTS

This mouse subspecies is found only on the Channel Islands. They are just a few inches long and have bulging eyes, much like their deer mouse cousins. You can find them climbing rocks, running through fields, or even swimming in streams.

PACIFIC GRAY WHALE
◯ 2 POINTS

Look out across the shoreline of this national park for the chance to see a Pacific gray whale. They have an incredible migration route, longer than any other mammal. They will sometimes travel from their mating grounds near Mexico to their feeding grounds by Alaska. For tips on where to see these giant beauties, ask a park ranger.

CALIFORNIA SEA LION ◯ 2 POINTS

These animals are known for their playfulness and intelligence, which is why you'll often see them at aquariums or in animal shows. People say they have dog-like faces with distinct snouts and whiskers. Their flippers are perfect for swimming in the ocean or having a little walk on land.

ISLAND SCRUB-JAY ◯ 2 POINTS

You can only find the island scrub-jay on Santa Cruz island. It does look a lot like other scrub-jays, though it is darker blue and has a distinct call. They are part of the crow and raven family, which means they are also known for their smarts. These bright and friendly birds are fun to see in the wild.

JOSHUA TREE
NATIONAL PARK

LOCATION Southern California
SIZE 789,000+ acres
FAMOUS FOR Joshua trees
ESTABLISHED 1994

6
NUMBER OF ITEMS

POINTS POSSIBLE
13

THE JOSHUA TREES GROWING throughout this national park look like something out of a children's book or sci-fi movie. They really do seem to take on a life of their own, twisting and turning in one direction and then another. As the closest national park to L.A., this one gets its fair share of visitors. The land is part of the Mojave desert, making up a unique ecosystem that is home to many birds, mammals, insects, and reptiles.

JOSHUA TREE ○ 1 POINT

Joshua trees aren't actually trees at all! They are related to yucca plants but have a tree-like growth habit. They only live at elevations of 2,000 to 6,000 feet, so their range is pretty limited. They are an important part of the Mojave ecosystem, providing food to area animals. If you happen to visit this national park at the right time (usually spring), you might even see them blooming.

GAMBEL'S QUAIL
○ 2 POINTS

This ground-dwelling bird is often found in desert areas. Both males and females have distinct tear-shaped plumes that hang over their forehead. The males also have other distinct markings like a brown cap on their head and creamy bellies whereas females are more gray overall.

CACTUS WREN ○ 2 POINTS

Cactus wrens look a bit like other wrens except their bodies are heavier overall and they have long, thick bills. They are often described as fearless, going where they please and being loud and vocal along the way. They frequently nest in cactus plants, a fun thing to look for as you hike through this national park.

DESERT TORTOISE
○ **3 POINTS**

Here's another national park where you can spot the desert tortoise. This large reptile isn't going to be easy to see because they can spend more than 90 percent of their time underground. However, it's always good to be on the lookout when you're out hiking.

WESTERN CHUCKWALLA
○ **3 POINTS**

The chuckwalla is an impressive member of the lizard family with limited range throughout the United States. This one can grow up to 16 inches long with about half of its length being tail. They like to seek shelter in rocks and other crevices, so keep an eye out if you're climbing up boulders.

SKULL ROCK ○ **2 POINTS**

Skull Rock is a famous hiking destination in Joshua Tree National Park. If you choose to hike the 1.7-mile loop, you'll be rewarded with a cool sighting of the rock that resembles a skull. This small trail is a great way to see many sights of this park.

PACIFIC NORTHWEST

WOLVERINE

WILD BERRIES

OLYMPIC CHIPMUNK

MOUNT RAINIER

NORTHERN SPOTTED OWL

CLARK'S NUTCRACKER

BLACK-TAILED DEER

OLYMPIC
NATIONAL PARK

LOCATION Northwest Washington
SIZE 922,000+ acres
FAMOUS FOR Temperate rainforests
and the Olympic Mountains
ESTABLISHED 1938

8
NUMBER OF ITEMS

POINTS POSSIBLE
18

THE LONG TRIP TO THIS NATIONAL PARK in the far northwest part of the United States will be worth it. One thing that makes this park so unique is all the different ecosystems you can experience. You'll find mountains, old-growth forests, oceans, rainforests, and so much more. This means there's a lot to see between waterfalls, plants, birds, and other wildlife. Better plan a few days for your trip to Olympic.

- -

ROOSEVELT ELK ○ 2 POINTS

There's a special kind of elk in Olympic National Park called Roosevelt elk. They are the largest elk in North America, with females weighing up to 700 pounds and males weighing more than 1,100 pounds. Here at Olympic, they like to hang out in the Hoh Rain Forest where they travel in groups of 20 or more. These large mammals are much bigger than the deer in the area, so you'll definitely know one when you see it. Males have antlers in summer and fall.

OLYMPIC CHIPMUNK ○ 2 POINTS

There's also a special kind of chipmunk you can find in this area. The Olympic chipmunk looks a lot like a regular chipmunk with brownish fur and light stripes. You won't find this little mammal anywhere else in the world. Like other chipmunks, it can store a lot of food in its cheek pouches as it moves it from one spot to another.

OLYMPIC MARMOT ○ 3 POINTS

There's yet another special mammal, which you can only find in this part of the world. The Olympic marmot is a rodent about the size of a cat with a bushy tail. Female marmots have up to six young (called pups) in their burrows in spring and then come out with them in summer. During cold months, they stay in their burrows to hibernate.

OLYMPIC TORRENT SALAMANDER

○ 3 POINTS

Salamanders aren't exactly easy to spot when you're out and about in a national park, but they offer a good challenge! While in Olympic, look for the Olympic torrent salamander, which likes to live in cool, damp areas. Like many salamanders, they have reduced lungs and so they do most of their breathing through their skin.

OTTER

○ 3 POINTS

There aren't many places where you can see both sea otters and river otters, but Olympic National Park is one of them! So how do you tell the difference? First of all, sea otters are much bigger than river otters. Also, they often float on their backs whereas river otters will swim on their bellies. The closer to the ocean you are in Olympic, the more likely you are to see a sea otter. But keep an eye out for both species whenever you see water in the park.

RAINFOREST ○ 2 POINTS

On the west side of Olympic National Park is the Hoh Rain Forest where more than 140 inches of rain falls every year. This is considered a temperate rainforest with lush, green canopies of moss and ferns. It's quite different than a tropical rainforest you might initially picture, but it's incredibly unique and full of life.

SAPSUCKER ○ 2 POINTS

While you're in Olympic National Park, keep an eye out for sapsuckers, which are a type of woodpecker. Here at the park, you'll find the red-naped and red-breasted sapsucker. Both woodpeckers nest in tree cavities. Then they'll drill holes in the trees to both eat the sap and to attract insects to the sap so they can eat those too.

HOT SPRINGS ○ 1 POINT

It's pretty amazing to think you can enjoy a hot tub made entirely by nature. Olympic National Park has two different hot springs you can visit: the Sol Duc Hot Springs and the Olympic Hot Springs. Both give you the opportunity to take a soak in warm water, completely surrounded by natural elements.

NORTH CASCADES
NATIONAL PARK

LOCATION Central Washington
SIZE 500,000+ acres
FAMOUS FOR Hiking trails with amazing views
ESTABLISHED 1968

5 NUMBER OF ITEMS

POINTS POSSIBLE 12

TRULY SET IN THE WILD, this national park is far less popular than other national parks in Washington, so you likely won't have to battle crowds or traffic to enjoy the wilderness here. Because of years of melting glaciers, there are lots of water activities like kayaking and fishing. It's also popular among those who enjoy camping in rugged conditions. Because of the remote atmosphere, there is a lot of wildlife to look for in this national park.

- -

WOLVERINE ○ 3 POINTS

Wolverines are incredibly cool mammals that often look different than a lot of people expect. They are a bit stocky and weigh up to 60 pounds. They can be up to 50 inches long, which includes a tail of up to 10 inches. They have very sharp claws that are always out, meaning they can't retract them on demand. Their feet grow to twice their typical size during winter, which helps them move around in the snow.

SALAMANDER ○ 3 POINTS

Any salamander you see in this national park should be considered a win because it can be hard to find them. In this park, you could see the long-toed salamander or the Pacific giant salamander. Both will be in cool, damp areas. Many salamanders will spend the majority of their lives in the water, and it's not until they are almost fully developed that they move onto land.

PIKA ○ 2 POINTS

You'll probably do a double take if you get the chance to see a pika because at first glance it resembles a little mouse. The pika is actually closely related to the rabbit, and is pretty soft ➡

and cuddly looking. Though pikas may be cute, these mammals are also quite tough. They can survive even in cold conditions by burrowing into the snow to stay warm and regulate their temperature.

BALD EAGLE ○ 2 POINTS

If you're near open water or a stream in this national park, look up because you might see an eagle nearby searching for its next meal. In the bird world, males are often bigger than females. However, this isn't the case for eagles. Females are around 25 percent bigger than males.

WILD BERRIES
○ 2 POINTS

Have you ever found strawberries growing in the wild? How about huckleberries? As you go along the trails of North Cascades National Park, challenge yourself to find wild berries. Of course, you should confirm for certain which berries they are before you try them, but it's a fun challenge to hunt for them regardless of whether you feel comfortable eating them.

it will continue to erupt in the future. If you want to go to Mount Rainier on a clear day, look up the forecast first. This will allow you to plan a great visit so when you get to the viewing spot, you'll be able to see for miles and miles!

WILDFLOWERS ○ 2 POINTS

The wildflower meadows around Mount Rainier are epic and bring people in year after year. You'll have to get the timing right—July and August is best—but if you do, you'll be rewarded with beautiful wildflowers as far as your eye can see. You've probably seen photos of this scene, and it's definitely worth checking out for yourself.

CLARK'S NUTCRACKER ○ 2 POINTS

Clark's nutcrackers are common mountain birds that are part of the crow and jay family, so they are smart! They are also large birds, up to a foot long. The males of this species are unusual in that they help the females incubate the eggs during nesting season. They also have a special pouch under their tongues, which helps them store seeds and nuts so they can transport them long distances.

CRATER LAKE NATIONAL PARK

LOCATION Southern Oregon
SIZE 183,000+ acres
FAMOUS FOR Deep lake with
clear blue waters
ESTABLISHED 1902

5 NUMBER OF ITEMS

POINTS POSSIBLE 10

AN ERUPTION more than 8,000 years ago formed this landscape. When Mount Mazama erupted it collapsed in on itself, creating a depression that filled with water to become this lake. Today, there are gorgeous cliffs all around the lake more than 4,000 feet high. The lake itself is nearly 2,000 feet deep, which makes it the deepest lake in the United States. Because of how the lake was created, there are no streams flowing in or out of it. This means means its water level is heavily dependent on variable rates of snowmelt, rainfall, and evaporation.

NORTHERN SPOTTED OWLS
◯ **3 POINTS**

The northern spotted owl is a subspecies of the spotted owl. They are about 1.5 feet tall with a nearly 4-foot wingspan. The females are larger than the males of this species, and owl couples will often mate for life. These owls have been listed as threatened in recent years, and they need us all to help with conservation efforts to make sure they will be here in the future.

MAZAMA NEWTS ◯ **3 POINTS**

What is a newt exactly? They are part of the salamander family, and they are considered semiaquatic. This means they mostly live on land, but they return to the water for mating. This specific newt is located in the Pacific Northwest, especially around Crater Lake. The best chance to see them is under rocks or driftwood near shorelines.

PHLOX ○ 2 POINTS

You can find plenty of wildflowers from spring through late fall at Crater Lake National Park. One of the earliest bloomers is phlox, which grows low to the ground and survives well even in mountainous areas. The little daisy-like blooms are such a bright spot in the wild.

BIKES ○ 1 POINT

Cyclists love biking around Crater Lake. It's a 33-mile ride all the way around, and it can be challenging even for people who bike regularly. If you're up for trying the ride yourself, you could look into bike rentals in the area. Otherwise, try to spot cyclists who are tackling the ride.

OVERLOOKS ○ 1 POINT

Since this national park overlooks a giant crater, there are no shortages of viewpoints here. The 33-mile loop road has lots of opportunities where you can snap beautiful photos. If you can time it right, try to make it to an overlook for sunrise, sunset, or even both. It's the perfect opportunity to capture that stunning vacation photo!

PACIFIC ISLANDS

HAWAI'IAN GOOSE

CRATER

'ŌHI'A TREE

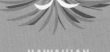

HAWAI'IAN SILVERSWORD

HAWAI'I VOLCANOES NATIONAL PARK

LOCATION The big island of Hawai'i
SIZE 330,000+ acres
FAMOUS FOR Volcanic landscape
ESTABLISHED 1916

6 NUMBER OF ITEMS

POINTS POSSIBLE **13**

THIS IS YOUR CHANCE to walk on an active volcano. Actually, there are two active volcanoes at this park, Kīlauea and Mauna Loa, and they are considered some of the world's most active! It's one of the most popular places in Hawai'i to visit, and many consider it a sacred place. Over the years, the lava these volcanoes have produced has reshaped the land in the area. Be sure to check out Crater Rim Drive, a loop that will take you to many of the key attractions at this park.

- -

'I'IWI HONEYCREEPER
○ 2 POINTS

You definitely won't miss this bird in the wild. The bright red bird with the long, curved bill is a common bird throughout Hawai'i, including this national park. It uses its bill to drink nectar from flowers. Over the course of more than 100 years, the bird's bill has actually shrunk. Scientists think this is because the flowers it drinks from have gotten shorter.

HAWKSBILL SEA TURTLE ○ 3 POINT

This sea turtle is named after its long, thin, hawk-like beak. They love tropical areas with coral reefs and they feed on sponges. It might be challenging to see one of these turtles in the wild because the males don't come to shore at all and the females only come to shore for nesting. However, a local expert or park ranger may have tips for how to see signs of this turtle.

'ŌHI'A TREE ◯ 2 POINTS
This tree and its signature red blossom is a common sight in
Hawai'i. The famous flower is called the lehua blossom, and legend
says if you pluck the flower from the tree, then it will rain on
the same day. The flower is quite popular, not only among birds,
butterflies, and insects who feed from the nectar, but also among
people who use it to make honey.

HAWAI'IAN SILVERSWORD ◯ 2 POINTS
This silversword is a rare and endangered plant that only grows
between 5,000 and 10,000 feet. The base of the plant is made up
of spiky greenish gray leaves. When this plant blooms, it sends up
this spectacular growth up to 6 feet tall. The plant can take years to
bloom, and then after it does it dies. So if you get the chance to see
this for yourself, know how incredibly rare it is!

LAVA ◯ 2 POINTS
There's no doubt you'll see
lava while at this national
park. It's just a matter of
whether it's cooled or not.
Lava can take more than 100
days to cool. Many people
come here in hopes of seeing
the glowing red lava you see
in movies or in photos. There
is a chance for this—check
with the local visitor's center.
Otherwise, ask a ranger to
point out the landscape that
is cooled lava. There's sure to be plenty of it!

FOSSIL ◯ 2 POINTS
Lava has preserved many fossils in the Hawai'ian landscape. If you
know where to look, you can see fossils of human footprints, birds,
trees, and more. To get tips of where to see fossils at this national
park, check with the visitor's center or a park ranger.

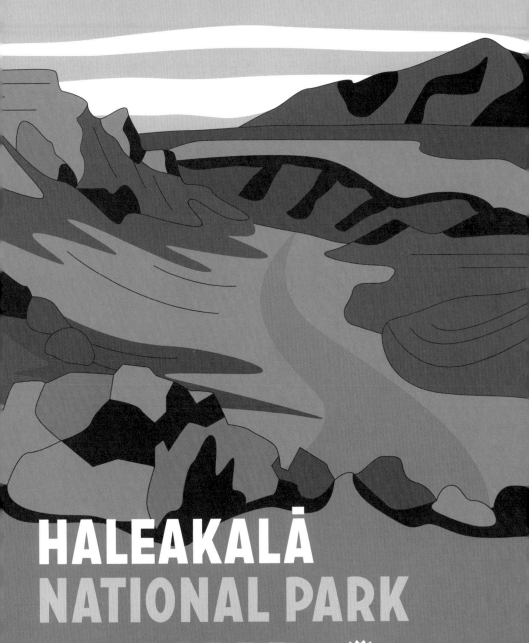

HALEAKALĀ
NATIONAL PARK

LOCATION Maui, Hawai'i
SIZE 29,000+ acres
FAMOUS FOR Diverse landscapes
ESTABLISHED 1916

5 NUMBER OF ITEMS

POINTS POSSIBLE **12**

A DORMANT VOLCANO called Haleakalā gives its name to this national park. The word also means "house of the sun." Many people will wake up well before dawn and drive to the famous Haleakalā Crater because they say this is one of the best places in the world to see the sunrise. There's so much variety in the landscape of this national park. In the area of the Haleakalā Summit, it looks like a barren planet. Then in lower Kīpahulu, it looks like a rainforest. If you ever find yourself in Maui, this park is a must-see destination.

HAWAI'IAN HOARY BAT ○ 3 POINTS

This bat, which became the state's official land mammal in 2015, is closely related to the North American hoary bat. It often roosts in trees and will come out at night to feed on moths, beetles, flies, and more. This bat is considered an endangered species, so consider yourself lucky if you get the chance to see it in person.

HAWAI'IAN MONK SEAL ○ 2 POINTS

This is one of the most endangered seals in the entire world, and Hawai'i is pretty much the only place you can see it in the wild. When the young (called pups) are born, they are completely black, and then they fade to a dark gray or brown. Ask locals where your best chance is to see this unique seal.

MAUI PARROTBILL

○ 3 POINTS

Here's another bird in the honeycreeper family that you can see while in Hawai'i. This parrotbill (also known as kiwikiu) has a large bill that looks like it belongs on a parrot. Because of its yellow and olive-green coloring, it looks like a cross between a canary and a parrot. This species is considered endangered, so it might be hard to spot. But this national park is one of the places it's possible.

CRATER ○ 2 POINTS

The Haleakalā Crater is an incredible sight, sitting more than 10,000 feet above the Pacific Ocean. This summit is the highest point in Maui, and the view is pretty amazing as you look down and see what has been created by nature.

HAWAI'IAN GOOSE

○ 2 POINTS

The Hawai'ian goose (also called the nene or nēnē) is the official state bird. It does have goose-like features that will probably be familiar, but you'll only find this bird in Hawai'i. They will often feed on ohelo berries, which are related to cranberries and grow on lava.

NATIONAL PARK OF
AMERICAN SAMOA

LOCATION 2,300 miles southwest of Hawaii
SIZE 9,000+ acres
FAMOUS FOR One of the wildest national parks
ESTABLISHED 1988

5 NUMBER OF ITEMS

POINTS POSSIBLE **12**

THIS IS THE FARTHEST most people will travel to a national park, but it's completely worth it. Made up of three islands, Tutuila, Ofu, and Ta'ū, this park is home to coral reefs, rainforests, and more. In fact, it's rare natural treasures like this that helped get this national park established. For instance, animals like the flying fox fruit bat now have protection thanks to conservation efforts around this park. This is the only American national park that is south of the equator, and it's steeped with Samoan culture. So put this park on your wish list if you want to learn about a different culture and see some rare, amazing sights.

- -

FLYING FOX FRUIT BAT ○ 3 POINTS

The fruit bat at this national park (also called the Samoan fruit bat) is a species within the flying fox family. It's one of the largest living bats, weighing up to 1 pound and with a wingspan of up to 2 feet. Their name comes from their fox-like face and the fact that most of their diet is fruit. They've been on the decline for years, so this national park is a safe space for them.

HUMPBACK WHALE ○ 2 POINTS

The humpback whale is one of the larger whale species, reaching up to 50 feet long and weighing up to 30 tons. It will often travel to the surface, making it a popular sighting for those on whale-watching trips. Male whales are known to have complex songs that will last up to 20 minutes.

RAINFOREST ○ 1 POINT

Many parts of the island are made up of tropical rainforests and tropical plants. This should give you the chance to see many rare and unique plants, including different types of ferns and flowers. Check with the visitor's center on what to look for during your trip.

WHITE-COLLARED KINGFISHER ○ 3 POINT

This kingfisher is roughly 9 inches long and has a large, distinct bill and beautiful teal-blue plumage. You'll often see them perched in trees or on wires, looking for their next meal. They will eat shrimp, crabs, and even a wide variety of insects. They are just one of the many tropical birds you can see while visiting this park.

BROWN BOOBY
○ 3 POINTS

Here's one more unique bird to look for while you're on the islands. This seabird is part of the booby family. It has large, webbed feet that are bright yellow and a long bill. These birds nest on the ground, often in groups, so if you find one nesting, you'll likely see more in the same area.

ALASKA

ORCA

STELLER SEA LION

NORTHERN HAWK OWL

MOUNT DENALI

GATES OF
THE ARCTIC
NATIONAL PARK

LOCATION Northern Alaska
SIZE 7.5+ million acres
FAMOUS FOR The northernmost
national park in the United States
ESTABLISHED 1980

6
NUMBER OF ITEMS

POINTS POSSIBLE
15

NOT ONLY IS THIS THE NORTHERNMOST national park in the country, but it's also some of the most wild, untouched land you can visit. You won't find roads, trails, or established campsites anywhere in this park, so you'll need to brush up on your backcountry skills before you venture into the wilderness. Since there are no roads, you either have to fly or hike to the park. Another great way to experience this land is to look for a tour or experienced guide to take you. This can be a great way to see all of Alaska's parks—through the eyes of a local! They will know where to find all of the best places and hidden treasures.

- -

CARIBOU ○ 2 POINTS

If you get the chance to see a caribou up close, pay attention to the way their bodies have adapted to deal with the snow and cold. They have long legs that help them travel through tall snowbanks. And their hooves are actually hollowed out, which helps them scoop up lichen underneath the snow.

ARCTIC FOX
○ 2 POINTS

In summer, Arctic foxes are brown or gray so they blend into the surrounding rocks and landscape. Then in winter, their fur turns bright white to help them blend into the snow! These foxes mate for life and will raise up to two litters each year.

MUSKOX ○ 3 POINTS

When you see muskox in the wild, it might feel like you're stepping back in time to the Ice Age. This enormous mammal, which grows up to 900 pounds, can be seen in parts of Alaska, including this national park. This animal is also known by the name Oomingmak, which means "hairy one" or "bearded one" in a local Yupik language.

NORTHERN LIGHTS ○ 3 POINTS

Gates of the Arctic is one of the best places to see the famous northern lights because it's so far north! Northern lights season tends to be best from September through April with the peak month being in March. Look online for a northern lights forecast to plan your opportunity to see this beautiful natural phenomenon.

NOATAK RIVER
○ 2 POINTS

This is one of the longest rivers in Alaska at more than 400 miles, and it runs through Gates of the Arctic. If you get the opportunity to experience the river for yourself, it can be an incredible place to watch wildlife, including bears, caribou, muskox, and more.

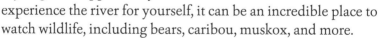

NORTHERN HAWK OWL ○ 3 POINTS

Is it a hawk or an owl? It really does look like a cross between the two, but it's in the owl family. Found exclusively in northern areas across the globe, they mostly hang out on their own but can sometimes be seen in pairs. While most owls are nocturnal, the northern hawk owl does the majority of its hunting during the day.

KOBUK VALLEY
NATIONAL PARK

LOCATION Northwest Alaska
SIZE 1.7+ million acres
FAMOUS FOR Scenery and sand dunes
ESTABLISHED 1980

5 NUMBER OF ITEMS

POINTS POSSIBLE **11**

KOBUK VALLEY IS ONE OF THE LEAST VISITED national parks, but this isn't because it lacks beauty or interest. It's just really tough to reach! With no roads leading into the park, you'll have to use a charter air taxi to get there. If you do make it, though, you will be rewarded with so many rare and epic sights. For example, caribou use this national park as a migration route. It's also home to some pretty spectacular sand dunes. All in all, this is another amazing, wild national park in Alaska, and it will not disappoint.

ARCTIC GROUND SQUIRREL ○ 3 POINTS

These are the biggest ground squirrels in North America at 14 to 18 inches tall, and they are also the squirrels that live farthest north. At first, it might look more like a groundhog or marmot than a squirrel, but they are definitely squirrels. They've adapted well to life in the North. Having thick fur and hibernating in their burrows 7 to 8 months out of the year helps them stay warm in this cold environment.

DUNE ○ 2 POINTS

The Great Kobuk Sand Dunes look a bit out of place in the Arctic, but they make up around 30 square miles in this national park. These sand dunes were created over time as the glaciers rubbed against the rocks to form fine sand.

KOBUK LOCOWEED
○ 2 POINTS

This is one of the only plants you can find in the Great Kobuk Sand Dunes. This little plant produces a beautiful purplish pink flower in summer months, and it's definitely a bright spot in this landscape. You have to visit Alaska at the right time to see this one, but it's definitely worth a photo.

CARIBOU

◯ **2 POINTS**

Did you know that the caribou is the only animal within the deer family where both males and females grow antlers? It's true! Females have smaller antlers and will shed them earlier than the males— usually after they give birth. But they both drop and grow new antlers every single year.

SNOWSHOE HARE ◯ **2 POINTS**

The snowshoe hare is a great animal to look for throughout your Alaskan adventures, and it will show up in this national park. It has large hind legs, which can look like the markings of a snowshoe, and its fur color varies based on the season. It's brown in the warmer months, and then it turns to a pure white in winter.

DENALI
NATIONAL PARK

LOCATION Central Alaska
SIZE 6.1+ million acres
FAMOUS FOR Home to North
America's tallest peak
ESTABLISHED 1917

7
NUMBER OF ITEMS

POINTS POSSIBLE

13

DENALI NATIONAL PARK promises visitors wilderness, adventure, and incredible natural sights. Home to the tallest mountain in North America, this park will make you feel the beauty and magic of being truly outdoors and in the middle of nowhere. It has forests, rocks, mountains, and so many wild animals. Nestled between two beautiful Alaskan cities, Fairbanks and Anchorage, it's one of the most accessible national parks in this state. Plan to spend several days exploring Denali because there is so much to see!

MOOSE ○ 2 POINTS
If you've had challenges seeing moose in the Lower 48, then head up to Alaska. More than 1,800 moose live in this national park. It's not uncommon to come across a moose mama and her babies (called calves) while just driving along the road.

CARIBOU ○ 2 POINTS
Did you know caribou and reindeer are the same animal? If you see a caribou in the wild, then know that you're looking at a real-life reindeer. These large mammals have an excellent sense of smell with hair that completely covers its nose. This helps them find food and vegetation, even under deep snow!

DALL'S SHEEP ○ 3 POINTS
Don't get Dall's sheep (also called Dall sheep) confused with a mountain goat, both of which you can see in this national park. For both Dall's sheep and mountain goats, males and females will have horns. However, mountain goats have slightly curved black horns while Dall's sheep have lighter horns that can sometimes curl into circles.

GRAY WOLF ○ 2 POINTS

Wolves can be a common sight in Denali if you know when and where to look. At first, you might think you're looking at a Husky sled dog, which you can also spot in this area, but wolves tend to be more slender overall. Wolves frequently hunt animals like moose and caribou, so they are often on the move looking for their next meal.

DOGSLED ○ 2 POINTS

Dogsled opportunities and tours are possible in this national park. Sled dogs have been present here for more than 100 years, and there's a deep history as to what they mean to this area and to the native people. Look into how to go for a ride through the park (mushing) or at least stop to visit some of the dogs in their kennel.

MOUNT DENALI ○ 1 POINT

Is it Mount McKinley or Mount Denali? It depends on who you ask because it's been a bit controversial over the years. It's officially Mount Denali (as of now), yet it's the same mountain either way. This is the tallest mountain in North America, reaching 20,320 feet. Roughly 1,000 people will try to climb this mountain every year, but only about half will succeed.

TRAIN ○ 1 POINT

Love the idea of traveling through a national park on a train? Then get your tickets for the Denali Star! This railroad has trains going through the national park every day. There's one track that goes south out of Fairbanks and another that goes north out of Anchorage. The train makes a few stops along the way, so it's the perfect way to see different parts of the park. Best of all, you can just sit back, relax, and watch for wildlife.

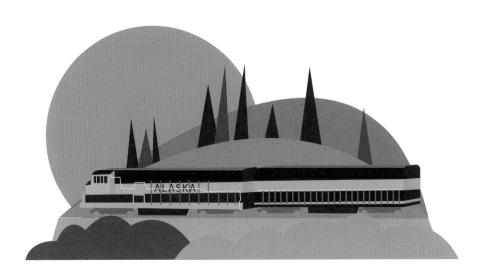

LAKE CLARK
NATIONAL PARK

LOCATION Southern Alaska
SIZE 2.6+ million acres
FAMOUS FOR Sockeye salmon
ESTABLISHED 1980

5 NUMBER OF ITEMS

POINTS POSSIBLE **11**

GLACIERS, RAINFORESTS, MOUNTAINS, AND VOLCANOES

—this national park has ties them all! You won't be able to drive to it since there are no roads going in or out, but you can reach it by boat or plane. Within the park, there are three rivers—the Chilikadrotna, Tlikakila, and Mulchatna—which are all designated as wild and scenic rivers or WSRs. They are all important in protecting this area's red sockeye salmon population as well as other fish.

SALMON ○ 3 POINTS

Scientists estimate that more than 300,000 salmon will swim upstream every year to enter this national park area. Sockeye salmon like the ones you will see here are born in freshwater and then they migrate out to the ocean. They will return to the freshwater where they were born before they spawn and die.

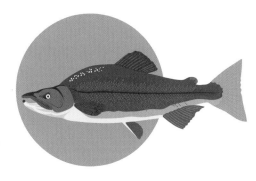

CANADA LYNX
○ 3 POINTS

Consider yourself lucky if you get a chance to see the Canada lynx in the wild. This lynx has distinct triangle-shaped ears with black on the tips, and large paws that act like snowshoes in the winter. They are great climbers and swimmers, so they do quite well throughout Alaska's wilderness.

RAINFOREST ○ 2 POINTS

Is there really a rainforest in Alaska? Within Lake Clark, there are temperate rainforests. Unlike tropical rainforests, these are forests with mild environments. They are often important in conservation efforts for area plants and animals, and they will help make your Alaska travels even more unique.

LAKE CLARK ○ 1 POINT

Lake Clark is the lake that makes up this national park, and it's where the salmon swim in and out of each year. It's about 40 miles long and includes amazing peaks, waterfalls, glaciers, and two nearby volcanoes. It's truly one of the most beautiful, largely untouched areas of Alaska.

VOLCANO ○ 2 POINTS

You might not even realize you're looking at a volcano when you see the ones in this national park. Both active volcanoes, Redoubt and Iliamna, sit over 10,000 feet and look a lot more like mountains than what you might be expecting of a volcano. This national park is located on what's called the Ring of Fire, one of the world's most active areas for earthquakes and volcanoes.

WRANGELL-ST.ELIAS NATIONAL PARK

LOCATION Eastern Alaska
SIZE 13 million acres
FAMOUS FOR Volcanoes and mountains
ESTABLISHED 1980

6
NUMBER OF ITEMS

POINTS POSSIBLE
13

IF YOU WANT TO SAY you've been to the largest national park in America, then start planning your trip here! At more than 13 million acres, this park could fit about six Yellowstone parks within it. It is home to four different mountain ranges—Wrangell, St. Elias, Chugach, and part of the Alaskan Range. Not surprisingly, it's also home to nine of the highest peaks in the United States. It's the perfect national park to visit if you want to escape everyday life and see nature up close. Plan your trip carefully and make sure you have the proper equipment. Then go see what the wildness of Alaska is all about!

PTARMIGAN ○ 2 POINTS

You can find two different species of ptarmigan birds in this national park: the willow and the rock. Both birds are members of the grouse family and have brownish coloring in summer and then change to all white plumage in winter.

MOOSE ○ 2 POINTS

There are several subspecies of moose in North America, including the Alaska moose. These are the largest moose with males weighing as much as 1,400 pounds and females weighing as much as 1,000 pounds. Male and female moose only come together to mate. Otherwise, they're pretty solitary. If you come across two moose, it's probably a young moose with its mom.

BEAVER ○ 2 POINTS

Do you know why beaver teeth are so cool? First of all, they are orange. Also, because they use them every day and they grind down quickly, they keep growing throughout their entire life. These teeth are an important part of their lifestyle in making their homes of dams.

TRUMPETER SWAN ○ 3 POINTS

This swan is the heaviest flying bird in North America, weighing in at 26 pounds. This is why you will often see them doing a running start across the water before they take off. You can find these birds in small pockets across North America, including a large area in Alaska.

FIREWEED ○ 2 POINTS

Fireweed is one of the most common wildflowers you'll find throughout Alaska in summer with its bright pink blooms. It often thrives in areas where other plants struggle to grow. In fact, it's often one of the first flowers to show up in an area after a fire. A lot of people see this as a sign of new life and rebirth.

MINE ○ 2 POINTS

Mining has been a big part of this area for years, and there are several abandoned mines in this national park. You'll want to avoid abandoned areas you might come across. However, if you want to get a feel for mining in the past, check out the Kennecott Mines National Historic Landmark.

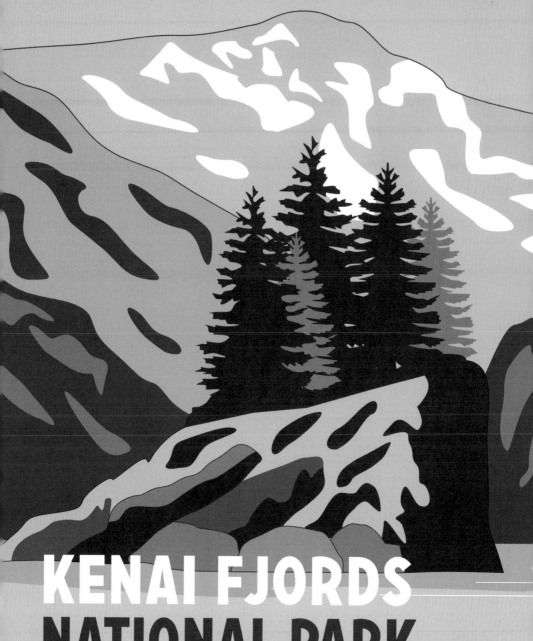

KENAI FJORDS
NATIONAL PARK

LOCATION Southcentral Alaska
SIZE 669,000+ acres
FAMOUS FOR Alaska wilderness
meeting the sea
ESTABLISHED 1980

6 NUMBER OF ITEMS

POINTS POSSIBLE **13**

OVER 40 GLACIERS form the Harding Icefield, protected by this national park. This is one of the only icefields left in the United States, and it's also the largest at more than 700 square miles. Kenai Fjords was named after the many fjords that exist here. Fjords are long, narrow inlets of ocean between really steep cliffs. They were carved by glacier activity, leaving behind beautiful scenery and landscapes. This park is tucked away in an area called the Gulf of Alaska, near the popular fishing town of Seward. You'll find plenty to see in this wild area.

- -

MOUNTAIN GOAT ○ 2 POINTS

These goats (which aren't goats at all but rather members of the antelope family) are fairly common here. Scientists estimate that more than 3,000 mountain goats live in this area, and in summer, you can often see them climbing the icefield. They will eat almost anything they can get ahold of, including grass, lichen, and other plants.

STELLER SEA LION
○ 3 POINTS

This is the largest sea lion, with males weighing up to 2,500 pounds and females weighing up to 800. They have a low-frequency voice, which means they sound more like they're roaring—other sea lions sound like they're barking. They've been on the endangered animal list in recent years, so you might want to ask locals for the best places to spot them.

PACIFIC WHITE-SIDED DOLPHIN ○ 2 POINTS

This dolphin (also known as the hookfin porpoise) has beautiful coloring, which you can easily spot as they're swimming through the ocean. They are known to be playful dolphins, and they often swim into cooler areas like this part of Alaska.

BLACK OYSTERCATCHER ○ 2 POINTS

The oystercatcher has pink legs and a bright red-orange bill. They are mostly black all over, though some will have some feathers that are brown or white as well. They like to hang out at rocky shores where they look for their latest meal of oysters, clams, mussels, and other shellfish.

HORNED PUFFIN ○ 3 POINTS

The horned puffin has the reputation of being a clown-like bird because of its colorful markings, similar to the Atlantic puffin. They will often live in colonies together, and they spend a lot of their days diving for fish for their next meal.

GLACIER ○ 1 POINT

Sometimes you don't even know you're looking at a glacier, but it's right there in front of you. Glaciers can even have names. Here at Kenai Fjords, some of the glaciers you could see include the Holgate, Grewingk, Aialik, and Exit Glacier.

KATMAI
NATIONAL PARK

LOCATION Southern Alaska
SIZE 3.6+ million acres
FAMOUS FOR Salmon and brown bears
ESTABLISHED 1980

5
NUMBER OF ITEMS

POINTS POSSIBLE
11

SALMON AND BROWN BEARS call this important protected wilderness home. Around 1912 a new volcano called Novarupta formed after a major eruption. A few years later in 1918, the area was designated as a national monument for its protection. Then the land was largely left untouched until the 1950s. This pristine land provided important habitat for the area, and it became a national park in 1980. Today this is one of the most active volcanic areas in the world, with at least 14 active volcanoes.

WHITE-CROWNED SPARROW ○ 2 POINTS

You have to be a tough songbird to make it in Alaska, and the white-crowned sparrow fits this description. This bird has a white-and-black striped head, and they travel far north into Canada and Alaska to raise their young each year. They eat insects almost exclusively.

BROWN BEAR
○ 2 POINTS

Scientists estimate that more than 2,000 bears live in this area, which actually outnumbers people who live here year-round. It's fairly easy to spot these bears while they're out and about fishing the streams, but it's always important to keep your distance. Remember—they are wild animals!

RED FOX ◯ 2 POINTS

Did you know the red fox lives on every continent in the world except Antarctica? It's true. These adorable mammals are pretty incredible to see in the wild. A fun fact about them is that they can retract their claws, much like cats can.

NORTHERN FUR SEAL ◯ 3 POINTS

These seals are part of the category of eared seals. They spend much of their lives out at sea, but they come to shore to rest, molt, and have more babies. Once the little ones (called pups) are weaned from their mothers, they will often spend up to two years out at sea before returning to the area where they were born.

SALMON ◯ 2 POINTS

If you go to Alaska, then try to time it for the chance to experience a salmon run. This is when thousands of salmon pass through an area in a short amount of time. This national park has one of the best salmon runs you can experience, and it really is amazing to watch.

GLACIER BAY
NATIONAL PARK

LOCATION Southeast Alaska
SIZE 3.2+ million acres
FAMOUS FOR Wilderness and scenery
ESTABLISHED 1980

5
NUMBER OF ITEMS

POINTS POSSIBLE
12

GLACIER BAY IS THIS BEAUTIFUL WILD LAND between the Gulf of Alaska and Canada. You will find more than 50 named glaciers in this park, including tidewater glaciers, as well as a wide range of animals, like bears, mountain goats, whales, moose, and more than 200 species of birds. Both large and small ships regularly go to Glacier Bay. In fact, many large cruise ships will come through to give passengers an up-close look at the Alaska wilderness.

- -

TIDEWATER GLACIER ◯ 2 POINTS

A tidewater glacier flows all the way down into the ocean. Ice regularly breaks away from these and makes a loud sound when it happens. They are impressive to see in the wild, and you can spot several at this national park.

DALL'S PORPOISE
◯ 3 POINTS

This porpoise is the largest species of its kind, growing up to 7.5 feet and weighing between 350 and 500 pounds. They often prefer cold water, which is why you could see them in the waters of Alaska. They tend to live in small groups of 10 or less but will sometimes gather with as many as 100 or more.

ORCA ◯ 3 POINTS

Orcas (also known as killer whales) grow up to 32 feet and weigh up to 6 tons. So essentially, they're about the size of a bus. These incredibly talented animals can live 50 to 80 years in the wild. Interesting fact: they aren't actually whales at all but instead are really dolphins.

TUFTED PUFFIN
○ 2 POINTS

Here's another puffin worth keeping an eye out for while in Alaska. The tufted puffin has a bright red bill and a bright white face. They often spend a lot of their time out in the ocean, but they come to shore to nest. Ask locals for tips on the best places to see them.

RAINFOREST ○ 2 POINTS

You probably don't usually think of glaciers and rainforests as existing in the same area, but they do here at Glacier Bay National Park. The southern part of the park has old-growth forests mixed with mild, moist climates. This makes it the perfect atmosphere for a temperate rainforest. Go see it for yourself!

ACKNOWLEDGMENTS

I'd like to give a big thanks to both of my kids, Jack and Annabelle, who were excellent sounding boards as I worked on this book. They even helped me research some unique facts along the way. In addition, I'd like to acknowledge the National Park Service's website, nps.gov. The National Park Service has a dedicated website for every single national park, and you can find so much good information on these sites. Since the park service is a nonprofit and a public resource, we should all be proud to have these resources at our fingertips. I use these sites frequently when planning my own trips to national parks, and I hope you utilize them as well.

Finally, I would encourage anyone going to a national park to stop off at the visitor's center and thank the park staff you come across. Many times, these are people who are there for the love of our public lands (not for the money), and we should all appreciate their role in preserving these resources for future generations.

SCAVENGER HUNT SCORECARDS

EAST NATIONAL PARKS	POSSIBLE POINTS	TOTAL POINTS
Acadia	24	
Shenandoah	23	
New River Gorge	12	
Cuyahoga Valley	10	
Indiana Dunes	12	
Gateway Arch	10	
Hot Springs	16	
Mammoth Cave	13	
Great Smoky Mountains	20	
Congaree	9	
Everglades	14	
Biscayne	12	
Dry Tortugas	11	
Virgin Islands	11	

MIDWEST NATIONAL PARKS	POSSIBLE POINTS	TOTAL POINTS
Voyageurs	14	
Isle Royale	8	
Theodore Roosevelt	9	
Badlands	11	
Wind Cave	10	

MOUNTAIN WEST NATIONAL PARKS	POSSIBLE POINTS	TOTAL POINTS
Glacier	24	
Yellowstone	24	
Grand Teton	16	
Rocky Mountain	15	
Great Sand Dunes	13	
Black Canyon of the Gunnison	11	
Mesa Verde	13	

CONTINUED ➡

SCAVENGER HUNT SCORECARDS

SOUTHWEST NATIONAL PARKS	POSSIBLE POINTS	TOTAL POINTS
White Sands	14	
Carlsbad Caverns	18	
Guadalupe Mountains	14	
Big Bend	18	
Saguaro	14	
Grand Canyon	18	
Grand Canyon	18	

UTAH AND NEVADA NATIONAL PARKS	POSSIBLE POINTS	TOTAL POINTS
Arches	12	
Canyonlands	13	
Capitol Reef	11	
Bryce Canyon	9	
Zion	16	
Great Basin	11	

CALIFORNIA NATIONAL PARKS	POSSIBLE POINTS	TOTAL POINTS
Redwood	12	
Lassen Volcanic	15	
Yosemite	17	
Kings Canyon	9	
Sequoia	11	
Death Valley	13	
Pinnacles	14	
Channel Islands	11	
Joshua Tree	13	

CONTINUED ➡

SCAVENGER HUNT SCORECARDS

PACIFIC NORTHWEST NATIONAL PARKS	POSSIBLE POINTS	TOTAL POINTS
Olympic	18	
North Cascades	12	
Mount Rainier	9	
Crater Lake	10	

PACIFIC ISLANDS NATIONAL PARKS	POSSIBLE POINTS	TOTAL POINTS
Hawai'i Volcanoes	13	
Haleakalā	12	
American Samoa	12	

ALASKA NATIONAL PARKS	POSSIBLE POINTS	TOTAL POINTS
Gates of the Arctic	15	
Kobuk Valley	11	
Denali	13	
Lake Clark	11	
Wrangell-St. Elias	13	
Kenai Fjords	13	
Katmai	11	
Glacier Bay	12	

STACY TORNIO is the author of more than fifteen books for families and kids, including *101 Outdoor Adventures to Have Before You Grow Up* and *The Kids' Outdoor Adventure Book*, both recipients of National Outdoor Book Awards. She is a former editor of *Birds & Blooms* magazine and currently runs the website BeAGoodHuman.Co, which encourages kids to take care of our planet.